IRAN: THE COMING CRISIS

I R A N:
THE COMING
CRISIS

MARK
HITCHCOCK

Multnomah® Publishers *Sisters, Oregon*

IRAN: THE COMING CRISIS
published by Multnomah Publishers, Inc.

Published in association with William K. Jensen Literary Agency, Eugene, Oregon
© 2006 by Mark Hitchcock

International Standard Book Number: 1-59052-764-X

Unless otherwise indicated, Scripture quotations are from:
New American Standard Bible © (NASB) © 1960, 1977, 1995 by the Lockman
Foundation. Used by permission.

Multnomah is a trademark of Multnomah Publishers, Inc.,
and is registered in the U.S. Patent and Trademark Office.
The colophon is a trademark of Multnomah Publishers, Inc.
Printed in the United States of America

For information:
MULTNOMAH PUBLISHERS, INC.
601 N. LARCH ST.
SISTERS, OREGON 97759

Library of Congress Cataloging-in-Publication Data
Hitchcock, Mark.
Iran : the coming crisis / Mark Hitchcock.
   p. cm.
ISBN 1-59052-764-X
   1. Bible—Prophecies—Iran. 2. Iran—History—Prophecies. 3. End of the
world. I. Title.
BS649.I73H57 2006
236'.9—dc22

                                    2006013982

06 07 08 09 10—10 9 8 7 6 5 4 3 2 1 0

DEDICATION

To Dr. John Walvoord,
whose writings and friendship have
profoundly impacted my life and ministry.

TABLE OF CONTENTS

PART THREE
IRAN'S FUTURE—THE FINAL JIHAD

INTRODUCTION

"An unrepentant rogue state with a history of sponsoring terrorists seeks to develop weapons of mass destruction. The United States tries to work with European allies to deal with the problem peacefully, depending on International Atomic Energy Agency inspections and United Nations sanctions. The Europeans are generally hesitant and wishful. Russia and China are difficult and obstructive. Eventually the reality of the threat, the obduracy of the rogue state regime in power, becomes too obvious to be ignored. This is not a history lesson about Iraq. These are today's headlines about Iran, where the regime is openly pursuing its ambition to become a nuclear power."[1]

WILLIAM KRISTOL, *THE WEEKLY STANDARD*

The eyes of the world are once again riveted on the Middle East, especially since the recent surge of militant, fundamentalist Islam in Iran. The meteoric rise of Iran to supremacy in that region has political leaders around the world filled with fear and trepidation. And, recently, the already bad situation in Iran has grown worse. Much worse. Since 2004 the world has watched as Iran has played a reckless game of nuclear hide-and-seek. For the first time, the world faces the threat of a rogue nation with an atomic arsenal. A rogue nation that supports terror and hates Israel and the West.

We face the terrifying threat of an atomic ayatollah—of nuclear jihad.

Of course, these developments present formidable economic, political, and military challenges for the U.S., Israel, and other Western nations. There are no easy solutions. Confrontation looms on the horizon.

But could the rise of Iran have even greater significance? Could it point toward the end-time scenario presented in the Bible?

I believe it does. The biblical prophecy in Ezekiel 38–39, written about 2,600 years ago, tells us that in the last days a great horde of nations will invade Israel while Israel is at rest in her own land. The leader of this invasion will be Russia, and one of the main allies in this confederation of nations, according to Ezekiel 38:5, is Persia—the modern nation of Iran.

Against all odds, from 1948 up to the present, the nation of Israel is being regathered to her land just as Ezekiel 37 predicted. In 2006 for the first time since AD 135, there are now more Jews in Israel than in any place on earth. Russia has risen to world prominence in the last century, and Iran is now world public enemy number one and an avowed anti-Semitic state. The current crisis in Iran and the Middle East is not the direct fulfillment of any biblical prophecy, but it is an ominous development that strikingly foreshadows what the Bible predicts. It points toward the fulfillment of the great prophecy of Ezekiel 38–39. The pieces of Ezekiel's prophetic puzzle seem to be coming together. It appears that the end-time stage is being set right before our eyes.

With this in mind, the main purpose of this book is to trace God's prophetic program for Iran: past, present, and future; to consider the ancient biblical prophecies of Persia (Iran's predecessor) that have already been fulfilled; to point out events we see today in the headlines related to the current crisis that seem to be setting the stage for the end times; and to gaze into Iran's future through the lens of Bible prophecy.

A PANORAMA OF PROPHECY

Going forward, it's important for you to have at least a basic knowledge of a few key biblical events in the end times. So, to make sure you understand these events, at the outset, let's do a brief review and define a few key terms that you will see sprinkled throughout the book.

The Rapture of the Church to Heaven

The Rapture is an event that, from our human perspective, could occur at any moment. It's what we might call a sign-less event. In other words, there's nothing that has to be fulfilled before this event takes place. It is truly imminent. At the Rapture, all who have personally trusted in Jesus Christ as their Savior, the living and the dead, will meet the Lord in the air and go with Him back up to heaven. Then, at least seven years later, they will return with Him, back to earth, at His Second Coming (John 14:1–3; 1 Corinthians 15:50–58; 1 Thessalonians 4:13–18).

The Seven-Year Tribulation Period

The Tribulation is the final seven years of this age. It will begin with a peace treaty between Israel and the Antichrist (Daniel 9:27). It will end with the Second Coming of Christ back to earth (Revelation 19). During this seven-year period, the Lord will pour out His wrath upon the earth in successive waves of judgment. But the Lord will also pour out His grace by saving millions of people during this time (Revelation 6–19).

The Three-and-a-Half-Year World Empire of Antichrist

At the midpoint of the treaty, the Antichrist will break it, invade Israel, and establish himself as world dictator. During the last half of the tribulation, Antichrist will rule the world politically, economically, and religiously. The entire world will give allegiance to him—or suffer persecution and death (Revelation 13:1–18).

The Campaign of Armageddon

The campaign or war of Armageddon is the final event of the great tribulation. It will occur when all the armies of the earth gather to come against Israel and attempt once and for all to eradicate the Jewish people (Revelation 14:19–20; 16:12–16; 19:19–21).

The Second Coming of Christ to Earth

The climactic event of human history is the literal, physical, visible, glorious return of Jesus Christ to planet earth. He will destroy the armies of the world, gathered in Israel, and will set up His kingdom on earth that will last for one thousand years (Revelation 19:11–20:6).

God's Blueprint for the End Times

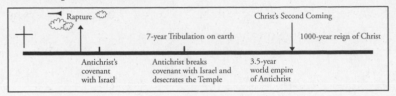

It's my prayer that this book will be used by God to help us see how history appears to be moving toward its climax and to attract every reader to our only Savior and Lord, Jesus Christ.

Mark Hitchcock

Edmond, Oklahoma

CHAPTER 1

THE GATHERING NUCLEAR STORM

How to handle Iran and, in particular,
its pursuit of nuclear weapons is a problem from Hell.
KENNETH POLLACK, *THE PERSIAN PUZZLE*

We're now at the dawn of an era in which an extreme
fanatical religious ideology, undeterred by the usual calculations
of prudence and self-preservation, is wielding state power and
will soon be wielding nuclear power.
CHARLES KRAUTHAMMER

The world today faces the greatest crisis in human history. Yes, you read it correctly. The world, right now, is facing its greatest crisis in six thousand years of recorded history. Greater than Nazi Germany.

Greater than Soviet communism.

The crisis officially began on January 9, 2006, when Iran broke the seals that International Atomic Energy Agency (IAEA) inspectors had placed on two nuclear plants and restarted its nuclear program. This broke a two-and-a-half year moratorium. The two offending Iranian nuclear plants were the Uranium Conversion Facility in Isfahan and the centrifuge plant at Natanz.[3]

When this occurred, the current crisis was officially on. The threat was triggered—the very real threat that Iran will get the bomb. That Iran's ayatollahs will go atomic. That Iran's incensed, anti-Semitic president, Mahmoud Ahmadinejad, could soon have his trigger finger on the button of an atomic weapon. That nuclear Weapons of Mass Destruction (WMDs) could be passed to terrorist groups who could detonate them on U.S. or European soil.

Some believe that Iran may already have a nuclear weapon. But most put the timetable for Iran's first weapon in one to four years. The Natanz plant has 164 centrifuges that have already been tested, and the plan is that in the fourth quarter of 2006 Iran will go to the next stage—three thousand centrifuges. There are plans to ultimately expand to 54,000 centrifuges. Iran's President, Mahmoud Ahmadinejad, has boasted that his nation is testing a centrifuge, known as P-2, that accelerates the creation of fuel for power plants or atomic weapons. The P-2 centrifuge quadruples the capacity of the P-1 centrifuge for enriching uranium.

Experts maintain that the Natanz plant in Iran could produce enough enriched Uranium for twenty-five weapons a year. At the same time Iran is pursuing its nuclear weapons program, Tehran also appears to be developing missiles capable of delivering atomic warheads. Iran has greatly increased production of Shahab-3 missiles, which it plans to arm with nuclear warheads. These missiles have a maximum range of about 2,000 kilometers (1,240 miles), which is the distance to Israel. In a secret program, code-named Project 111, Iran's "aim is arming Shahab-3 missiles with nuclear warheads."[4]

Iran has also received its first shipment of North Korean-made surface-to-surface missiles known as BM-25. These missiles have a range of 1,550 miles, putting Europe within fir-

THE GATHERING NUCLEAR STORM   17

ing range, and are capable of carrying nuclear warheads. The BM-25s are a significant upgrade over its existing top-of-the-line Iranian missiles—the Shahab-4 and Shahab-3. Iran's action on January 9 was the final straw for the Europeans, primarily Britain, France, and Germany, who had been negotiating with Iran for over two years concerning its nuclear intentions.[5] And Israel, already on highest alert, quickly concluded that Iran had reached a point of nuclear no return.

The U.S. began to immediately condemn Iran's actions and speak of the "grave threat." Iran quickly moved to the top of the list of U.S. foreign policy.

But most surprisingly, even the French, who are known for their extreme caution, quickly responded to the new crisis. On January 19, 2006, French President Jacques Chirac warned that, "Leaders of states who would use terrorist means against us, just like anyone who would envisage using, in one way or another, arms of mass destruction, must understand that they would expose themselves to a firm and fitting response from us.... This response could be conventional. It could also be of another nature." He added that there should be no doubt "about our will and our capacity to use nuclear arms." Chirac even hinted that France had already retargeted its nuclear arsenal.[6]

Within hours of this announcement, Iran responded by declaring that it would withdraw an estimated $30 billion to $50 billion in cash reserves from European banks. Also, oil prices on the world market quickly spiked to over $70 a barrel, and the New York Stock Exchange fell 2 percent.

Then, in February 2006, Iranian scientists successfully restarted four centrifuges necessary to produce weapons-grade uranium. Iranian officials blocked access to international inspectors and disabled security and surveillance cameras put in place by the International Atomic Energy Agency (IAEA) thirteen years ago when Iran first admitted to violating the nuclear nonproliferation treaty.

Iran now has access to its own uranium ore and all the essential infrastructure for weapons-grade plutonium production. And it's quite possible that Iran could acquire fissile material from a black market source that would greatly accelerate its production of a nuclear weapon.

On April 9, 2006, a major milestone was reached. Iran began enriching uranium. Iranian President Mahmoud Ahmadinejad said, "I am officially announcing that Iran has joined the group of countries which have nuclear technology. At this historic moment, with the blessings of God almighty and the efforts made by our scientists, I declare here that the laboratory-scale nuclear fuel cycle has been completed and young scientists produced enriched uranium needed to the degree for nuclear power plants Sunday." He also said, "I formally declare that Iran has joined the club of nuclear countries." At the celebration in honor of this landmark, Iran staged a celebration with dancers brandishing capsules of uranium hexaflouride gas. Ahmadinejad said, "Our answer to those who are angry about Iran obtaining the full nuclear cycle is one phrase, we say: Be angry and die of this anger."

Some optimistically maintain that Iran is several years away from possessing a nuclear weapon. However, in March 2006, the United States alleged that Iran already has enough uranium gas to make ten nuclear weapons.

The real question is—when will we reach the point of no return? And, could this mounting crisis be a flashing sign of the end times?

THE LOOMING CONFRONTATION

Of course, Iran insists that its nuclear plans are civilian only and has no other purpose than to generate power. However, it's now generally agreed that Iran has embarked upon a course that can have no other plausible intent other than to produce nuclear weapons.

Iran has a twenty-year history of deception in the nuclear issue. Graham Allison, in his bestselling book, *Nuclear Terrorism*, says: "Iran is today the leading example of a country that is simultaneously exploiting the current nonproliferation regime and sneaking around it.... Iran is a serial confessor, successively owning up to the facts when its accusers have unambiguous evidence, while hiding what is yet to be found. Through a combination of legal and illegal actions, it now stands at the threshold of a nuclear weapon."[7]

However, both the U.S. and Israel have made it crystal clear that a nuclear Iran is unacceptable. The Bush administration has repeatedly and clearly stated that they can not and will not allow Iran to possess nuclear weapons. Robert G. Joseph warns that "Iran is at the nexus of weapons of mass destruction and terrorism" and that "if Iran has fissile material or nuclear weapons, the likelihood of their transfer to a third party would increase."

In March 2006, the Bush administration released a forty-nine-page foreign policy doctrine. In that document they said that Iran and its nuclear ambitions are the biggest future challenges to the U.S. The document stated, "We face no greater challenge from a single country than from Iran. We will continue to take all necessary measures to protect our national and economic security against the adverse consequences of their bad conduct."

However, some in America naively believe that a nuclear

Iran can be effectively contained. In an op-ed piece in *The New York Times*, Barry R. Posen maintains that a nuclear Iran could be easily managed by the U.S. He argues that "aggressive, even reckless" actions by Iran aren't inevitable. He believes that Iran would not pass nuclear devices to terrorists because they could be traced back to Iran and that Iran would then face nuclear attack by the West.[8]

But most people strongly disagree. The Bush administration has repeatedly stressed that we cannot allow Iran to obtain nuclear weapons. President Bush has called the Iran crisis a "grave national security concern." On January 30, 2006, on CBS's *Face the Nation*, President Bush said, "Our strategy is to present and hold together a united front to say to the Iranians, 'Your designs to have a nuclear weapon or your desire to have the capability of making a nuclear weapon is unacceptable.'"

Yuval Steinitz, the chairman of Israel's Foreign Affairs and Defense Committee has said, "It is now clear the race began again and time is running out." And yet Iran stubbornly claims that nuclear capability is their right. They say that the present path is irreversible.

On June 12, 2004, Iranian foreign minister Kamai Kharrazi said, "We won't accept any new obligation. Iran has a high technical capability and has to be recognized by the international community as a member of the nuclear club. This is an irreversible path."

On March 14, 2006, Ayatollah Ali Khamenei, Iran's supreme leader, said that Iran's nuclear fuel program is "irreversible." He said that "any retreat at this point will bring an unending chain of pressures and further retreats."

A senior Iranian official said, "Iran's nuclear activities are like a waterfall which has begun to flow. It cannot be stopped."

Something has to give.

There's every indication that Iran is on a collision course with Israel and the West. The nuclear showdown has begun. Iran is a ticking nuclear time bomb. The world stands at the precipice of a potential nuclear nightmare. Iran is on the path to build weapons to blow Israel off the map. Confrontation looms on the horizon. The U.S. and other Western nations or Israel will eventually act to take out the nuclear facilities. It takes no great imagination to see how this crisis could easily spark a chain of events leading to the final war of Armageddon.

IRAN RISING

How did the world get to this point? What has triggered Iran's bold moves? Why has Iran chosen to make the nuclear move now?

Ever since the 1979 Islamic revolution, when the Ayatollah Khomeini and his followers overthrew the government, Iran has been a fundamentalist, radical Islamic nation with its mind set on *jihad*, or holy war, against all non-Muslim infidels. Iran's direct support of terrorism is just one of the many proofs of Iran's serious commitment to *jihad*. Iran is the only Shiite Muslim state in the world. About 90 percent of Muslims worldwide are Sunni, but Iran is the only Muslim nation that has adopted Shiite Islam as its state religion.

Since 1991, five key events have led to Iran's rise to a position of power in the Muslim world, emboldening her to take the final, nuclear step.

First, the mighty Soviet empire came apart in 1991. Middle East experts agree that communism was the greatest

FAST FACTS ABOUT IRAN

Name:	Islamic Republic of Iran
Population:	68 million
Area:	1.648 million square km.
Government:	Theocratic Republic
Administrative Divisions:	30 provinces
Capital:	Tehran (7 million population)
Religion:	Islam (90 percent Shiite, 9 percent Sunni)
Official Language:	Persian or Farsi

MILITARY ARSENAL

540,000	active soldiers (estimated)
350,000	reserves (estimated)
120,000	Revolutionary Guards
undetermined number	Shahab missiles with a range of 1,500 miles
about 12	Russian-made Scud missile launchers
2,000	Tanks
Hundreds	Helicopters
300	Combat aircraft
3	Submarines

control and constraint on fundamentalist, radical Islam. With the fall of the Soviet Union, this impediment has been removed and Iran now practices and propagates her brand of radical religion throughout the entire region, thereby wielding tremendous religious and political influence.

Second, the war in Iraq has crippled the military machine of Iran's archenemy. As menacing a threat as Saddam Hussein was, the one benefit of his power was that he helped hold Iran

THE GATHERING NUCLEAR STORM   23

in check. In 1980, a border dispute between Iran and Iraq erupted into a war when Iraqi troops invaded Iran. The war continued until 1988, when Iran and Iraq agreed to a cease-fire. During this prolonged war, Iran and Iraq kept one another distracted and weak enough that the rest of the world was essentially safe from their threats and terrorism. The Iran-Iraq War ended in 1988, and then the government of Saddam Hussein was toppled in 2003. Iran is now left as the great Middle East menace. Iran is now world public enemy number one, especially for Israel and the West.

Third, with the ongoing conflict in Iraq and an over-stretched U.S. military, Iran knows that the United States and the West have less capacity to react and are, therefore, very reluctant to escalate the situation. The United States is suffering a credibility gap due to the absence of WMDs in Iraq and already has its hands full in its peacekeeping capacity there. If serious action is taken against Iran, they could retaliate by turning Iraq into a bloodbath by fueling the Sunni-Shiite division that is already at the boiling point. A full-fledged civil war in Iraq would be disastrous for the West.

Fourth, Iran recognizes that the West is dependent on oil and will do almost anything not to disrupt the fragile oil supply line. Iran lies along the Persian Gulf and could cripple world supply by several means at her disposal.

Fifth, Iran is counting on the fact that its extensive commercial ties with Russia and China will insulate it from any punitive measures from the U.N. Security Council. These five factors have come together and given Iran what it believes is the perfect time and ideal opportunity to act. It may also be God's time to pave the way for the beginning of the end.

THE REALLY BAD NEWS

So how serious is the current crisis? How bad could a nuclear Iran be? With the presence of WMDs in the wrong hands, the myriad of doomsday scenarios is nothing short of terrifying.

The Senate Foreign Relations Committee surveyed analysts around the world in late 2004 and early 2005 to ascertain what they believed was the potential threat posed by weapons of mass destruction. The study was commissioned by committee chairman Senator Richard Lugar. He released this statement. "The bottom line is this: For the foreseeable future, the United States and other nations will face an existential threat from the intersection of terrorism and weapons of mass destruction."

Employing a poll of eighty-five nonproliferation and national security experts, the report estimated the risk of attack by weapons of mass destruction would be as high as 70 percent within the next ten years.

The report from the survey also contained these findings:

- Most of the more than eighty experts surveyed believed one or two new countries will acquire nuclear weapons in the next five years, with two to five countries joining the nuclear club during the next decade.

- The most significant risk of a WMD attack was from a radiological weapon, or a so-called "dirty bomb," in which radioactive material is put into a conventional explosive device. The threat of such a device being detonated somewhere in the world over the next decade was set at 40 percent.

- The next highest risk was of an attack with a chemical or biological weapon, with a nuclear attack judged least likely.

- The likelihood of a WMD attack in the next five years is rated at 50 percent.

- The risk of a nuclear attack over the next five years is 16.4 percent.[9]

We are only five years into the age of terror, and just think what we've already seen. Think of Iran and her allies in the world-terror network. Just imagine what could loom on the near horizon. Make no mistake. The threat is real. The consequences are staggering. The time could be any day. And such a cataclysmic event could easily trigger a series of military and economic actions and reactions that would bring us to the door of the end times.

Time could be running out before the coming of Christ.

DISCERNING THE SIGNS OF THE TIMES

In Matthew, Jesus rebuked the self-righteous Jewish leaders for their blindness to the signs of the times. Jesus was performing signs all around them that fulfilled Old Testament prophecies and proved that He was the long-awaited Messiah.

The Pharisees and Sadducees came up, and testing Jesus, they asked Him to show them a sign from heaven. But He replied to them, "When it is evening, you say, 'It will be fair weather, for the sky is red.' And in the morning, 'There will be a storm today, for the sky is red and threatening.' Do you know how to discern the appearance of the sky, but cannot discern the signs of the times?" (16:1-3)

At Jesus' first coming, the nation of Israel as a whole was blind to the many signs all around them that the Messiah had come. The Old Testament had clearly prophesied many things concerning the Messiah's person and works. Yet, the people failed to put it all together. Why? Because many of them were ignorant of the prophetic word, or just didn't take the time and effort to really understand what it was saying.

People back then weren't a whole lot different from most people today. They wouldn't have thought of missing the evening weather on the news, but they totally neglected the Word and what it said about the signs of the times. The people in Jesus' day missed the clear signs of His first coming. Likewise, many today are oblivious of the signs of His Second Coming.

What's clear from Jesus' words is that He expects us to discern the signs of the times *whenever* we live, and understand what time it is in terms of what matters most.

Let us consider how to stimulate one another to love and good deeds, nor forsaking our own assembling together, as is the habit of some, but encouraging one another; and all the more, as you see the day drawing near (Hebrews 10:24–25).

Obviously, we have to be looking for Christ's coming to carry out this exhortation. After all, how in the world can we ever hope to "see the day drawing near" if we aren't even looking for it, or have no idea what we are looking for?

Of course, we should never engage in wild speculation or set dates for Christ's coming. But we should do the best we can to understand the signs of the times. To determine as best we can the season in which we live. Jesus calls us to investigate the prophecies of the Bible and know our times.

Undoubtedly, one aspect of our times that we need to consider from the perspective of Bible prophecy is the current crisis in the Middle East, focused on Iran. This crisis is politically, economically, and militarily supercharged. We're all aware that it's unlike anything the world has ever faced. It involves all of the world's most combustible ingredients: radical Islam, oil, Israel, China, Russia, and the West. Iran's actions and alliances currently being formed and solidified look like they were taken directly out of the biblical prophecy found in Ezekiel 38–39.

One would be very hard-pressed to find another time in history when there was more at stake—or when the major prophetic signposts were lined up pointing to the end.

Now is the moment, if there ever was one, to "discern the signs of the times."

However, before we look at the present developments in Iran and her prophetic destiny, let's look very briefly at what God's Word has to say about Iran's predecessor, the mighty Persian Empire. The precision of the biblical prophecies concerning the Persian Empire and their exact fulfillment provide an important backdrop for Iran's present and the biblical prophecies concerning her future.

PART ONE

IRAN'S PAST—THE PERSIA PROPHECIES

The Bible is a book of prophecy. Most people probably don't realize that, at the time it was written, 28 percent of the Bible was prophetic in nature. Many of these prophecies were fulfilled within a few years of the time they were given, some were fulfilled centuries later, and many others still await fulfillment.

It's important to look at the biblical prophecies that have already been fulfilled for two main reasons. First, they prove that the Bible is true. No other book in human history foretells the future with 100 percent accuracy, 100 percent of the time. The Bible is batting a thousand when it comes to predicting the future.

Second, the fulfillment of past prophecies establishes an unbroken pattern of literal fulfillment. All of the biblical prophecies that have already been fulfilled were fulfilled literally. With this kind of precedent established, we can expect that the future, unfulfilled prophecies will also be literally ful-filled.

Some of the biblical prophecies that have already been ful-filled deal with the ancient Persian Empire, the predecessor of modern Iran. Let's look briefly at these amazing "Persia Prophecies" that have already been fulfilled and use them as a springboard to the present and future.

CHAPTER 2

HISTORY'S SILVER KINGDOM

In its day, the Persian Empire was a superpower like nothing the world had ever seen—with a monotheistic religion, a vast army, a rich civilization, a new and remarkably efficient method of administration, and territory stretching from Egypt to Central Asia.

KENNETH POLLACK, THE PERSIAN PUZZLE

The predecessor of the modern nation of Iran was Persia—a mighty empire that ruled the world of its day for a span of about two hundred years. The name was officially changed to Iran in March 1935. The Iranian people know the history of their nation and it's a source of enormous pride, even arrogance, for them.

The history of Persia is important from a cultural and political standpoint, but also from a biblical one. Most people probably are unaware that the words *Persia*, *Persian*, and *Persians* occur thirty-five times in the Old Testament. These words occur in only five books in the Old Testament: 2 Chronicles, Ezra, Esther, Ezekiel, and Daniel.

While the Bible certainly has something to say about Iran's future destiny, as we will see later, the vast majority of the references to Persia in the Bible deal with the mighty Persian Empire that ruled the world from 539 to 331 BC. The references to the Persian Empire in 2 Chronicles, Ezra, and Esther are all simply historical statements concerning the ancient Persian Empire. The Book of Daniel, however, records prophecies that were future in Daniel's day concerning the coming of the Persian Empire. Therefore, Daniel is the key book in gaining a clear understanding of the rise and fall of the mighty Persian Empire.

Winston Churchill once said, "The farther backward you can look, the farther forward you are likely to see." With this maxim in mind, let's look back to the very beginning of the Persian Empire, so we can better understand what's happening today and see as far as possible into the future of Iran.

THE HEAD OF GOLD

There's an old Chinese proverb that says, "It's difficult to prophesy, especially about the future." We know this all too well. No man knows what will happen tomorrow, tonight, or even today, let alone next year.

God's Word is absolutely clear that only God knows the future (Isaiah 41:21–23; 44:6–7). In fact, this is one of the major proofs that the Bible is the Word of God. It foretells future events with 100 percent accuracy, 100 percent of the time.

One of the great prophecies in the Bible is found in Daniel 2. It's often called the ABCs of Bible prophecy. In this chapter, the Jewish prophet, Daniel, was given a revelation by God that revealed not just the next day or the next one hundred days, but what now has been more than 2,500 years. Of course, Daniel was not given every detail. But he was shown the major flow of world history from his own day, in about 550 BC, until the second coming of Jesus Christ to earth, to rule and reign forever. His incredible prophecy is as relevant today as it was the day it was written.

NEBUCHADNEZZAR'S NIGHTMARE

Daniel 2 opens in the year 602 BC, in Babylon. At that time the great Babylonian monarch, Nebuchadnezzar, was probably in his late 20s. He was the ruler of the world. But he was restless. As the old saying goes, "Uneasy lies the head that wears the crown."

Nebuchadnezzar's forces undertook several military expeditions from 604–602 BC. Egypt still remained a formidable opponent and was not finally subjugated until 570 BC.

One night in 602 BC, young Nebuchadnezzar was lying in bed thinking about his future and the future of his empire (Daniel 2:29). He had seen other nations destroyed, even by his own hand. He had probably witnessed the fall of Nineveh just a few years earlier, in 612 BC.

During the night, God responded to Nebuchadnezzar's desire by revealing the future to him in a dream that greatly troubled and perplexed him. When he awoke, Nebuchadnezzar knew that this dream was significant. He was so anxious to know its meaning that he called in all his counselors and advisors very early in the morning. He demanded that they do two things: (1) give him the content of his dream and (2) interpret its meaning. The wise men of Babylon were not especially wise—but they knew enough to argue that no man could do what the king asked. No king had ever asked such a thing before! Filled with fear, they reluctantly confessed total inability to meet the king's demand.

The Chaldeans answered the king and said, "There is not a man on earth who could declare the matter for the king, inasmuch as no great king or ruler has ever asked anything like this of any magician, conjurer or

Chaldean. Moreover, the thing which the king demands is difficult, and there is no one else who could declare it to the king except gods, whose dwelling place is not with mortal flesh."

Because of this the king became indignant and very furious and gave orders to destroy all the wise men of Babylon. So the decree went forth that the wise men should be slain; and they looked for Daniel and his friends to kill them. (Daniel 2:10–13)

Many people believe that Nebuchadnezzar had forgotten the dream and wanted his advisers to give him the dream for that reason. I don't think so! I believe he remembered the dream vividly. He asked his advisers to give him the dream and its interpretation knowing that, if they could give him the dream, their interpretation would be trustworthy. Anyone can offer an "interpretation" of a dream. But telling someone the content, too, is humanly impossible. If you can do the impossible, your interpretation must be true.

In his anger, Nebuchadnezzar issued the "Dunghill Decree." If they could not give him the dream and the interpretation, they would be torn limb from limb and their homes would be reduced to rubbish, or dung heaps.

This certainly grabbed their undivided attention.

DANIEL AND THE DREAM

Since Daniel and his three Hebrew friends were part of Nebuchadnezzar's inner circle of counselors, they were covered by this edict as well. So Daniel interceded with Arioch, the king's bodyguard, for a brief stay of execution. As a result of this conversation, Daniel actually went in before Nebuchadnezzar to ask for more time (Daniel 2:14–16). Nebuchadnezzar was in no mood for delaying tactics, but there must have been something in the eyes of this young Hebrew man that captivated the king. There was some kind of calm assurance that led the king to give a brief reprieve.

Knowing that time was short, Daniel called his friends together for a prayer meeting to ask God to give them the information they needed to stay alive (Daniel 2:17–18). That night, in a vision, God revealed to Daniel both the dream and its interpretation.

Now, the natural response would be to rush in immediately before the king to give him the good news. But before going in, Daniel paused to bless the God of Heaven—to give God the glory for giving him the revelation (Daniel 2:19–23).

The next morning, Daniel was led in before Nebuchadnezzar. In your mind you can just picture the scene. Nebuchadnezzar was seated on his throne—afraid, frustrated, and angry. He had no expectations that Daniel could do what none of his other charlatans were able to do.

Daniel first began by openly giving God all the credit for the revelation he had received and was about to reveal. He made it clear that he was just a mouthpiece used by the God of Heaven. Daniel then proceeded to tell Nebuchadnezzar what he was thinking about before he went to sleep the night he had the dream. "As for you, O king, while on your bed your thoughts turned to what would take place in the future" (Daniel 2:29).

At this point you can imagine how Nebuchadnezzar must have scooted forward on his throne with his mouth hanging open. Then, in one of the most dramatic episodes in the Bible, Daniel recounted Nebuchadnezzar's dream.

> "You, O king, were looking and behold, there was a single great statue; that statue, which was large and of extraordinary splendor, was standing in front of you, and its appearance was awesome. The head of that statue was made of fine gold, its breast and its arms of silver, its belly and its thighs of bronze, its legs of iron, its feet partly of iron and partly of clay.
>
> You continued looking until a stone was cut out without hands, and it struck the statue on its feet of iron and clay and crushed them. Then the iron, the clay, the bronze, the silver and the gold were crushed all at the same time and became like chaff from the summer threshing floors; and the wind carried them away so that not a trace of them was found. But the stone that struck the statue became a great mountain and filled the whole earth. (Daniel 2:31–35)

Then Daniel, without missing a beat, began to unveil the meaning of the dream.

> "This was the dream; now we will tell its interpretation before the king. You, O king, are the king of kings, to whom the God of heaven has given the kingdom, the power, the strength and the glory; and wherever the sons of men dwell, or the beasts of the field, or the birds of the sky, He has given them into your hand and has caused you to rule over them all. You are the head of gold.

"After you there will arise another kingdom inferior to you, then another third kingdom of bronze, which will rule over all the earth. Then there will be a fourth kingdom as strong as iron; inasmuch as iron crushes and shatters all things, so, like iron that breaks in pieces, it will crush and break all these in pieces. In that you saw the feet and toes, partly of potter's clay and partly of iron, it will be a divided kingdom; but it will have in it the toughness of iron, inasmuch as you saw the iron mixed with common clay. As the toes of the feet were partly of iron and partly of pottery, so some of the kingdom will be strong and part of it will be brittle. And in that you saw the iron mixed with common clay, they will combine with one another in the seed of men; but they will not adhere to one another, even as iron does not combine with pottery.

In the days of those kings the God of heaven will set up a kingdom which will never be destroyed, and that kingdom will not be left for another people; it will crush and put an end to all these kingdoms, but it will itself endure forever. Inasmuch as you saw that a stone was cut out of the mountain without hands and that it crushed the iron, the bronze, the clay, the silver and the gold, the great God has made known to the king what will take place in the future; so the dream is true and its interpretation is trustworthy." (Daniel 2:36–45)

What did all this mean?

THE MEANING OF THE METALLIC MAN

The four metals in the great statue represented four great empires that would appear successively on the world scene to rule over the civilized world of that day. In the hindsight of history we now know that these four empires were Babylon, Medo-Persia, Greece, and Rome. The feet and the ten toes of iron and clay point forward, even from our day, to a final, ten-king form of the Roman empire.

The great stone cut out without hands, which destroys the great statue, is Jesus Christ. He will come at His Second Coming as a Smiting Stone who will destroy The Antichrist and his kingdom and then set up His own Kingdom that will fill the whole earth.

Five Kingdoms

Gold	BABYLON
Silver	MEDO-PERSIA
Brass	GREECE
Iron	ROME
Iron & Clay	KINGDOM OF ANTICHRIST

The Metallic Man of Daniel 2

WORLD EMPIRE	DESCRIPTION
Babylon	Head of Gold
Medo-Persia	Chest and Arms of Silver
Greece	Belly and Thighs of Brass
Rome	Iron
Rome II (Antichrist's Kingdom)	Feet and Ten Toes of Iron and Clay
Christ's Kingdom	Stone Kingdom that fills the earth

Historically, Nebuchadnezzar and Babylon were the great head of gold on the image. Babylon heads up the list of empires that are opposed to God and His people, Israel.

Babylon, under Nebuchadnezzar, terminated the Davidic kingship and was the first nation to subjugate Jerusalem. The Babylonians came against Jerusalem three times, ultimately destroying the Jewish temple in 586 BC.

The Babylonian empire under Nebuchadnezzar thrived and prospered. He constructed the beautiful hanging gardens for his homesick wife. These became known as one of the Seven Wonders of the Ancient World.

The historian Herodotus visited Babylon about 100 years after Nebuchadnezzar, and reported that he had never in his life seen such a proliferation and abundance of gold. One statue of the god Marduk alone weighed 22 tons (that's 44,000 pounds!) of solid gold.

Truly, Babylon was history's head of gold.

FROM GOLD TO SILVER

The fact that the Babylonian empire, according to God's plan, was destined to be replaced by another empire lets anyone reading Daniel know that Babylon had to fall. The head of gold had to give way to the chest and arms of silver.

In the fifth chapter of his own book, Daniel describes the transfer of world power from Babylon to the Medo-Persian empire in 539 BC. On Saturday night, October 12, 539 BC, Nebuchadnezzar's grandson, Belshazzar, was having a big Babylonian bash. At one point in the feast, in his drunken bravado, he ordered the gold vessels taken from the temple in Jerusalem almost fifty years earlier to be brought into the hall and filled with wine for his guests. This was a direct affront, a direct challenge, a clear, ill-considered assault on the God of Heaven. And Belshazzar got more than he bargained for. Much more.

As he stood near his throne, honoring his false gods and mocking the true God, a heavenly hand suddenly appeared out of nowhere, in the light of the lampstand, and began to write on the plaster of the king's wall. Belshazzar turned ashen and his knees literally began to knock together. "Then the king's face grew pale, and his thoughts alarmed him; and his hip joints went slack, and his knees began knocking together" (Daniel 5:6).

I would think so!

The divine finger of fate wrote four simple words on the palace wall: MENE, MENE, TEKEL, UPHARSIN.

No one had any idea what these words meant. But someone remembered the old man Daniel, who would have been about eighty years old by this time. Daniel was brought in and delivered God's message of judgment to Belshazzar and

Babylon. He rebuked Belshazzar for not learning from his grandfather's punishment. (Nebuchudnezzar was made like a beast of the field for seven years—see Daniel 4:1–37.) And then, after indicting him for his pride, arrogance, and failure to glorify God, Daniel interpreted the Divine handwriting on the wall.

MENE, MENE	Numbered, Numbered
TEKEL	Weighed
UPHARSIN	Divided

God's message to Belshazzar was as straightforward as a slap across the face. "Belshazzar, your number is up, you do not measure up, and your kingdom is to be broken up."

The night of revelry and revelation turned into a time of retribution. For that very night, the Medo-Persians broke into the city by means of an ingenious plan. The Euphrates river flowed through Babylon, so they dug a huge canal and diverted the water, allowing their soldiers enough room to get under the massive wall. Once the soldiers got under the wall, some helpful soul from the inside (thinking perhaps that they were Babylonian soldiers who had fallen off the wall) opened the gate into the city. The soldiers flooded in and Belshazzar was slain that very night. God's judgment was swift. Babylon's time was up! The kingdom passed to the Medo-Persian empire (Daniel 5:31).

History's head of gold was finished, and the silver kingdom moved to center stage.

WHY SILVER?

The silver kingdom in Nebuchadnezzar's dream represented the ancient Persian Empire. The two arms of silver represent the original twofold division of the empire into the Medes and the Persians.

One fact that is interesting to consider in regard to parts of the image is why God used silver to represent the Persian empire?

Gold was the symbol for the Babylonian empire because this kingdom was dominated by gold. Just as Babylon was the Golden Kingdom, Persian was the Silver Kingdom. The Persians instituted a complicated postal system and a vast system of taxation in which the taxes were paid in silver. In Aramaic, the word for silver and the word for money were synonymous. The Persians acquired vast hordes of silver. They literally stuffed their coffers with silver. Taxes from the twenty provinces controlled by Persia yielded three and a half million pounds of silver per year.

At the time when Alexander the Great invaded Persia, even after Darius III had used much silver in the war with Alexander and carried off half a million pounds of silver, Alexander plundered twelve to eighteen million pounds of silver from the Persian cities of Susa, Persepolis, and Pasargadae.

Ancient Persia was the silver kingdom!

WHEN BRONZE BEAT SILVER

The mighty Persian Empire ruled the world from 539 BC until it fell in 331 BC to the Greek Empire ruled by Alexander the Great. At that time the silver kingdom gave way to the bronze kingdom according to God's predetermined plan.

But there's more.

The prophet Daniel has more to say about the ancient Persian empire.

CHAPTER 3

VISIONS OF PAST GREATNESS

*Today's Iran is culturally ancient and demographically
young—a combustible compound.
It nurses nostalgia about vanished Persian grandeur.*
GEORGE WILL

In Daniel 2, the nightmare of Nebuchadnezzar pictured five world empires that would rule the world. The second of these empires was ancient Persia.

Daniel 7–8 zeroes in on these same empires but presents them in a totally different way.

THE JUNGLE BOOK

In Daniel 7, the prophet has a vision at night in which he saw four terrible beasts coming up out of the sea. These four beasts corresponded to the four metals of the image in Daniel 2, and the ten toes on the image in Daniel 2 correspond to the ten horns on the fourth beast in Daniel 7.

Here's the text, with a summary interpretation in the table immediately following:

In the first year of Belshazzar king of Babylon Daniel saw a dream and visions in his mind as he lay on his bed; then he wrote the dream down and related the following summary of it. Daniel said, "I was looking in my vision by night, and behold, the four winds of heaven were stirring up the great sea.

"And four great beasts were coming up from the sea, different from one another. The first was like a lion and had the wings of an eagle. I kept looking until its wings were plucked, and it was lifted up from the ground and made to stand on two feet like a man; a human mind also was given to it. And behold, another beast, a second one, resembling a bear. And it was raised up on one side, and three ribs were in its mouth between its teeth; and thus they said to it, 'Arise, devour much meat!'

"After this I kept looking, and behold, another one, like a leopard, which had on its back four wings of a bird; the beast also had four heads, and dominion was given to it. After this I kept looking in the night visions, and behold, a fourth beast, dreadful and terrifying and extremely strong; and it had large iron teeth. It devoured and crushed and trampled down the remainder with its feet; and it was different from all the beasts that were before it, and it had ten horns. While I was contemplating the horns, behold, another horn, a little one, came up among them, and three of the first horns were pulled out by the roots before it; and behold, this horn possessed eyes like the eyes of a man and a mouth uttering great boasts. (Daniel 7:1–8)

The Beasts of Daniel 7

EMPIRE	DESCRIPTION
Babylon	Lion with the wings of an eagle
Medo-Persia	Lopsided bear with three ribs in its mouth
Greece	Leopard with four wings and four heads
Rome	Terrible Beast with teeth of iron and claws of bronze
Rome 2 (Kingdom of Antichrist)	Ten Horns and the Little Horn

Now consider the obvious parallels between the metals of Daniel 2 and the beasts of Daniel 7:

Parallels Between Daniel 2 and 7

WORLD EMPIRE	DANIEL 2	DANIEL 7
Babylon	Head of Gold	Lion with the wings of an eagle
Medo-Persia	Chest and Arms of Silver	Lopsided Bear with three ribs in its mouth
Greece	Belly and Thighs of Bronze	Leopard with four wings and four heads
Rome	Iron	Terrible Beast with large iron teeth
Rome 2 (Reunited Roman Empire)	Iron and Clay (10 toes)	10 Horns and Little Horn

THE BLOODTHIRSTY BEAR

In Daniel 7:5, the ancient Persian empire is pictured as a lopsided, devouring bear with three ribs in its mouth.

This chapter covers the same ground as Daniel 2, but there

are two significant changes. First, in Daniel 7 more detail is given. One of the important principles to remember in interpreting Daniel is that Daniel presents the same themes repeatedly, adding more detail each time.

Second, in Daniel 2 world empires are presented from man's point of view in the form of a beautiful, stately image constructed of precious metals. However, in Daniel 7, the same empires are presented as four wild, ravenous beasts: a lion with wings like an eagle, a bear with three ribs in his mouth, a leopard with four heads and four wings, and a fourth dreadful, terrible beast with great iron teeth and ten horns. H. A. Ironside, a well-known Bible teacher, notes the significance of these changes.

> In what we have already gone over we have chiefly occupied with prophetic history as viewed from man's standpoint; but in the second half of the book we have the same scenes as viewed in God's unsullied light. In the second chapter, when a Gentile king had a vision of the course of world-empires, he saw the image of a man—a stately and noble figure—that filled him with such admiration that he set up a similar statue to be worshipped as a god. But in this opening chapter of the second division, Daniel, the man of God, has a vision of the same empires, and he sees them as four ravenous wild beasts, of so brutal a character, and so monstrous withal, that no actual creatures known to man could adequately set them forth.
>
> There is something exceedingly solemn in this. If you read history as viewed simply by the natural man, you will find that a great deal of space is given to con-

gratulating humanity upon their marvelous exploits; and one would suppose that we have now almost reached perfection, so far as human government or political economy is concerned. Civilization and the progress of the race are presumably at the zenith of their glory. But if one reads history in the light of Holy Scripture, with the Spirit of God illuminating the page, it gives one a very different impression indeed. We then begin to realize that the things that are most highly esteemed among men are abominations in the sight of God.[10]

The Persian Empire that was represented by the chest and arms of silver in Daniel 2 is represented by a bear raised up on one side with three ribs in his mouth in Daniel 7. The focus in this symbol is on conquest. With heavy, plodding, bear-like progress the Persian Empire conquered the world. The bear is lopsided or raised up on one side to symbolize the early domination of the Median part of the empire that was later overshadowed by Persian influence. The three ribs in the bear's mouth represent the remains of the three most important nations Persia conquered: Lydia (modern Turkey), Babylon, and Egypt.

Ancient Persia was a bloodthirsty bear!

THE TWO-HORNED RAM

Daniel 2 and 7 focus on five world kingdoms that will precede the coming of Jesus Christ to earth to rule and reign. In Daniel 8, however, the focus narrows to two of the world empires, Medo-Persia and Greece, symbolized by two beasts, a ram and a male goat.

In the third year of the reign of Belshazzar the king a vision appeared to me, Daniel, subsequent to the one which appeared to me previously.

I looked in the vision, and while I was looking I was in the citadel of Susa, which is in the province of Elam; and I looked in the vision and I myself was beside the Ulai Canal.

Then I lifted my eyes and looked, and behold, a ram which had two horns was standing in front of the canal. Now the two horns were long, but one was longer than the other, with the longer one coming up last.

I saw the ram butting westward, northward, and southward, and no other beasts could stand before him nor was there anyone to rescue from his power, but he did as he pleased and magnified himself.

While I was observing, behold, a male goat was coming from the west over the surface of the whole earth without touching the ground; and the goat had a conspicuous horn between his eyes.

He came up to the ram that had the two horns, which I had seen standing in front of the canal, and rushed at him in his mighty wrath.

I saw him come beside the ram, and he was enraged at him; and he struck the ram and shattered his two horns, and the ram had no strength to withstand him. So he hurled him to the ground and trampled on him, and there was none to rescue the ram from his power.

Then the male goat magnified himself exceedingly. But as soon as he was mighty, the large horn was broken; and in its place there came up four conspicuous horns toward the four winds of heaven. (Daniel 8:1–8)

In the vision, the ram symbolizes Persia and the goat symbolizes Greece. This identification is confirmed in Daniel 8:20–21: "The ram which you saw with the two horns represents the kings of Media and Persia. And the shaggy goat represents the kingdom of Greece: and the large horn that is between his eyes is the first king."

The first beast that appears in Daniel 8 is a ram. However, this ram had an unusual characteristic—one of its horns was higher than the other, and the higher horn was the one that came up last. This represents the fact that in the Medo-Persian Empire, the Median part of the empire was originally dominant, but was later surpassed by the Persian element of the empire. This is similar to the one side of the bear being higher than the other in Daniel 7.

Media was a major power as early as 612 BC when they helped Nebuchadnezzar defeat Assyria and conquer Nineveh. At that time Persia was small, with holdings of only 50,000 square miles. When Cyrus came to power, he began to conquer surrounding nations and gained control over Media in 550 BC, which was about the time of this vision in Daniel 8. Thus, Persia became the greater of the two empires, and with the two empires consolidated, Cyrus moved on to establish the vast Medo-Persian Empire.

The fact that the Persian Empire is represented by a ram in Daniel 8 is important. In battle, the Persian ruler bore the golden figure of a ram's head as he stood at the head of his army. Ram's heads are on the sculptured pillars of Persepolis. Persian coins had a ram's head on one side. In that day, different lands had signs of the zodiac to represent them and the sign for Persia was Aries, the ram. In the *Zendevesta,* Ized Behram, the guardian spirit of Persia, appears like a ram with cloven feet and sharp pointed horns. The ram was the symbol for ancient Persia!

The activities of the ram are amazing, especially when one remembers that Daniel recorded these words in 550 BC before these events occurred. The ram pushed westward, northward, and southward. Note that Daniel does not say that the ram pushed eastward.

This was fulfilled with exact precision because Persia was on the eastern edge of the empire and never pushed to the east. However, Persia did push westward into Babylon, Syria, and Asia Minor, northward into Armenia and the Caspian Sea area, and southward into Egypt and Ethiopia. Cyrus conquered in every direction with great ease. As Daniel 8:4 says, "no other beasts could stand before him nor was there anyone to rescue from his power; but he did as he pleased and magnified himself."

CYRUS THE GREAT

The ease with which Cyrus was able to conquer other nations is a matter of history. After consolidating Media and Persia he moved across northern Mesopotamia to Asia Minor almost unopposed. There he defeated a wealthy king named Croessus. He then marched back east to Babylon, which he took without a battle (Daniel 5:25–31). As Daniel said, "he did as he pleased and magnified himself."

One of the most amazing prophecies in the Bible is found

in Isaiah 44:28–45:6, where Isaiah called Cyrus, the great Persian king, by name and gave the details of his conquests—150 years before he was born!

> "It is I who says of Cyrus, 'He is My shepherd! And he will perform all My desire 'And he declares of Jerusalem, 'She will be built,' And of the temple, 'Your foundation will be laid.'" Thus says the LORD to Cyrus His anointed, whom I have taken by the right hand, to subdue nations before him and to loose the loins of kings; to open doors before him so that gates will not be shut: "I will go before you and make the rough places smooth; I will shatter the doors of bronze and cut through their iron bars. "I will give you the treasures of darkness and hidden wealth of secret places, so that you may know that it is I, the LORD, the God of Israel, who calls you by your name. "For the sake of Jacob My servant, and Israel My chosen one, I have also called you by your name; I have given you a title of honor though you have not known Me. "I am the LORD, and there is no other; besides Me there is no God. I will gird you, though you have not known Me; that men may know from the rising to the setting of the sun that there is no one besides Me. I am the LORD, and there is no other.

Up to this point in the vision, all the focus is on the ram, and then suddenly the scene is interrupted by the appearance of a male goat or, literally, "a buck of the goats."

THE ANGRY GOAT

According to Daniel 8:21, the goat in Daniel's vision is the Greek Empire and the ruler of this empire, symbolized by the large horn, is Alexander the Great. Interestingly, Greece viewed Persia as a ram, and the Persians viewed Greece as a goat. The astrological sign for Greece was Capricorn, the one-horned goat. The national emblem of Macedonia was a goat. According to tradition, Caremus, the first Macedonian king, was directed by an oracle to take a goat for a guide and build a city where he was led. He did this and followed a herd of goats to Edessa, which he made his capital, changing its name to Egaea—the goat city. The emblem of a goat was found on many Greek coins, and the Aegean Sea that borders Greece is literally "the Goat Sea." Also, Alexander's son by his wife Roxana was named Aegus, which means "son of a goat." The goat was Greece and the big horn was its first king, Alexander the Great.

In 334 BC Alexander departed from Pella with thirty-five thousand troops to cross the Hellespont to avenge the Persian invasion of Greece 150 years before, under the Persian monarch Xerxes. Alexander left Greece at the age of twenty-two, never to return.

Alexander's first battle against the Persians was at the Granicus River in May 334 BC where he routed Darius III. The second time Alexander engaged the Persians was at Issus in November 333 BC. The Persians had an army of 600,000 against Alexander's army of 35,000; however, the Persians were once again defeated and Darius' mother, wife, and children were captured, but he escaped. Alexander met the Persians for the final time at Guagamela or Arbela in October 331 BC. In this battle, Persia was crushed!

Daniel 8:7 was exactly fulfilled: "I saw him come beside the ram, and he was enraged at him; and he struck the ram and shattered his two horns, and the ram had no strength to withstand him. So he hurled him to the ground and trampled on him, and there was none to rescue the ram from his power." The great Persian ram was totally subjugated and stomped in four years.

In 330 BC, Alexander went on to sack and plunder the main cities of the Persian Empire: Susa, Persepolis, and Ecbatana. In Susa, as the final act of total conquest, Alexander seated himself on Darius' throne beneath its famous golden canopy—an act that meant death for anyone other than its legitimate occupant.

Thus, the Persian Empire was brought low and went the way of all flesh!

FROM BC TO AD

The ancient Persian Empire ruled the world for two hundred years in power and human splendor as the silver kingdom, the bloodthirsty bear, and the two-horned ram. But, in 331 BC, her splendor was ruined by the Greek Empire, which is represented by the bronze kingdom in Daniel 2, the four-headed leopard in Daniel 7, and the male goat in Daniel 8.

After Persia's demise, she passed off the scene as a major power and eventually deteriorated into a second rate nation with little power or prestige in the world. However, in the last thirty years that situation has been dramatically reversed. Today, Iran is the major player in the Middle East.

The rise of Iran is a key stage-setting event for the events of the end times. Iran must become a key player in the Middle

East for the ancient prophecy of Ezekiel 38 to be fulfilled.

For this reason, we must now turn our attention from the past to the present—from Persia's past rule to her present rise in the nation of Iran.

From 331 BC to AD 2006.

KEY DATES IN PERSIAN HISTORY RELATED TO THE OLD TESTAMENT

550 BC	Cyrus the Great rose to power over the Medo-Persian Empire.
October 12, 539 BC	Medo-Persians overthrew of the city of Babylon just as Daniel predicted in Daniel 5.
538 BC	King Cyrus allowed the Jewish people to return to Israel, ending the 70-year Babylonian captivity.
480–473 BC	Esther married King Xerxes, and the story in the Book of Esther unfolded in Persia
March 444 BC	King Artaxerxes allowed Nehemiah to return to Israel to rebuild the walls of Jerusalem and restore the city.
334–331 BC	Persia overwhelmed by Alexander the Great in a series of crushing defeats as predicted in Daniel 8.

PART TWO

IRAN'S PRESENT—
SHADOWS OF COMING EVENTS

All of us have been outside on many occasions and looked down to see our shadow on the pavement in front of us.

Of course, we all know that our shadow is not us. It's not our substance. In some ways it resembles us, but in many other ways, not at all.

Yet it is a sign.

For instance, when you see Mark Hitchcock's shadow, you can count on the fact that Mark Hitchcock is near at hand. It's a sign that I am coming. (Not very quickly, perhaps, especially if I'm jogging, but with great certainty!)

In the same way, coming events often cast their shadows upon this world before they arrive, functioning as what we know as "signs of the times." It's happening right now as you read these words. Future events are casting their shadows before them. The shadows seem to be everywhere, but nowhere are they more evident than in the current crisis in the Middle East.

Let's look at some current shadows that are casting their darkness across the earth, and as we look at them, remember that the substance may not be far behind.

CHAPTER 4

THE MOTHER OF MODERN TERROR

Depending on your own beliefs, Ahmadinejad is either mystical or deranged. In either case, he is exceedingly dangerous. And Iran is just the first. With infinitely accelerated exchanges of information helping develop whole new generations of scientists, extremist countries led by similarly extreme men will be in a position to acquire nuclear weaponry. If nothing is done, we face not proliferation, but hyperproliferation. Not just one but many radical states will get weapons of mass extinction, and then so will the fanatical and suicidal terrorists who are their brothers and clients.

CHARLES KRAUTHAMMER

I n the January 30, 2006, issue of *U.S. News and World Report*, Mortimer B. Zuckerman pulled no punches when he described the state of Iran:

Iran today is the mother of Islamic terrorism. Tehran openly provides funding, training, and weapons to the world's worst terrorists, including Hezbollah, Hamas, the Palestinian Islamic Jihad, and the Popular Front for the Liberation of Palestine, and it has a cozy relationship with al Qaeda. It has given sanctuary to major al Qaeda terrorists, including senior military commander Saif al-Adel, three of Osama bin Laden's sons, and al Qaeda spokesman Suleiman Abu Ghaith. It supports many of the barbaric terrorists in Iraq who are murdering innocent civilians in order to destroy Iraq's fragile hold on democracy. Through its 900-mile border with Iraq, Iran is flooding its neighbor with money and fighters. It is infiltrating troublemakers into Afghanistan, supporting terrorism against Turkey, sustaining Syria, and had a hand in the Khobar Towers bombing in Saudi Arabia.[11]

How did this come about? How did Iran become the mother of modern terror?

BIRTH OF A MODERN NATION

The modern nation of Iran began in 1921 with a man named Reza Khan, who led the Cossack Brigade. On February 21, 1921, he brought his Cossack Division into Tehran and by 1923 he was installed as the new shah. He took the name Reza Shah Pahlavi. During his tenure, Reza Shah focused on modernization and industrialization. He was fascinated with the rise of Germany in the 1930s and considered the Persians a fellow Aryan state with Germany. The name was changed from Persia (land of the Parsa) to Iran (land of the Aryans) in 1935.

THE ISLAMIC REVOLUTION AND THE HOSTAGE CRISIS

Fast-forwarding about forty years, in the late 1970s several facts converged that made the climate ripe for revolution in Iran. Ruhollah Musavi Khomeini, a 70-year old mullah, burst onto the troubled scene. He became the founding father of the modern Iranian state. Gary Sick describes him like this. "Khomeini was the archetype of the medieval prophet emerging from the desert with a fiery vision of absolute truth." Khomeini's vision was appealing because it "held the answers to all questions, and the answers were absolute and final."[12] Khomeini held a magnetic appeal over many segments of Iranian society, and he was obsessively opposed to the United States. He repeatedly referred to the U.S. as the "Great Satan."

On Valentine's Day 1979, 150 members of a Marxist group attacked and overran the U.S. Embassy in Tehran. But the attack was quickly denounced by Ayatollah Khomeini, probably because the attackers were godless Marxists. However, on November 4, 1979, a group of about 300 Islamist students attacked and overran the U.S. embassy. This time Khomeini supported the action since these students were his loyalists. Sixty-six American diplomats and Marines were taken hostage. Fourteen were later released, but the remaining fifty-two hostages were held for 444 days and suffered physical and psychological abuse.

This was Iran's first direct attempt to strike a blow against the "Great Satan" and humiliate the hated superpower.

FOUNDING AND FUNDING TERROR

Iran today is at the center of the worldwide terror network. The Teheran Conference in Iran, in 1991, was attended by radical Islamic movements and terrorist groups from at least forty countries. At this conference the attendees declared themselves to be against making any kind of peace with Israel. Since that time, Iran has developed a very cozy relationship with al Qaeda, has helped found, and is an ardent supporter of, Hezbollah, or the Party of God, that terrorizes Israel on a

KEY DATES IN IRAN'S HISTORY

March 21, 1935	Name changed from Persia to Iran.
1978–79	Islamic Revolution under Ayatollah Ruhollah Khomeini.
January 16, 1979	Shah of Iran fled the country.
February 11, 1979	Final overthrow of the Shah's government.
April 1, 1979	Name changed to Islamic Republic of Iran.
November 4, 1979	U.S. embassy in Tehran seized and 52 hostages taken. Crisis lasted 444 days.
September 22, 1980	Iraq invaded Iran beginning an eight-year war, resulting in half a million to a million casualties.
January 1995	Russia signed an $800 million nuclear plant deal with Iran to complete the nuclear plant at Bushehr.
November 2004	Iran agreed to suspend uranium enrichment.
August 2005	Mahmoud Ahmadinejad won the election in June and was installed as President of Iran in August.
November 2005	Russia signed deal with Iran for $1 billion worth of missiles and other defense systems.
January 9, 2006	Iran rebuffed European diplomatic efforts and resumed uranium production at its plant in Natanz claiming that its only intention was to make reactor fuel to generate electricity.
February 11, 2006	The 35-member International Atomic Energy Agency voted to report Iran to the UN Security Council over its resumed atomic program.
March 8, 2006	The IAEA, meeting in Vienna, voted to refer Iran to the UN Security Council.
March 29, 2006	The UN Security Council unanimously approved a statement demanding Iran suspend uranium enrichment.
April 9, 2006	Iran officially announced that it had begun enriching uranium.

regular basis, and openly funds, trains, and provides weapons for the world's nastiest terrorists such as Hamas, the Palestinian Islamic Jihad, and the Popular Front for the Liberation of Palestine. Iran supports the barbaric terror groups in Iraq and infiltrates terrorists into Afghanistan, and funds and supports at least a dozen terror groups around the globe.[13] Iran has done everything in its power to derail any peace talks or agreement between Israel and the Palestinians including a $50 million gift to the terror group Hamas, which now runs the Palestinian government.

KHOBAR TOWERS

The Khobar Towers was a housing complex in eastern Saudi Arabia for American troops who defended Saudi Arabia and contained Iraq after the Gulf War. On June 25, 1996, a huge truck bomb exploded at the Khobar Towers obliterating half of an entire building. The explosion killed nineteen Americans and wounded 372. A group known as Saudi Hizballah was behind the operation. But it was soon discovered that this organization was created by the Iranian Revolutionary Guard.[14]

The U.S. had strong evidence that Iran was behind the attacks, but as is often the case in these incidents, the evidence was insufficient to hold up in an international court of law.

The attack on the Khobar Towers was Iran's first direct terrorist attack against the U.S., but not the last. On May 12, 2003, three truck bombs were detonated in Riyadh, Saudi Arabia in Western housing complexes. The explosions killed twenty people, including seven Americans. Intelligence reports later revealed that the attacks were orchestrated by al Qaeda with connections to Iran.

THE KATRINE A INCIDENT

You might also remember the huge shipment of Iranian arms headed to the Gaza Strip that was commandeered in the Red Sea by the Israelis in early 2002. The Palestinian ship, named the *Katrine A*, was seized by Israeli naval commandos in the Red Sea, 300 miles south of Eilat on January 3, 2002. The shipment contained fifty tons of weapons destined for the Palestinian Authority, which at that time was under the control of Yasser Arafat. Among the fifty tons of weapons were machine guns, mines, mortars, Katyusha rockets, rocket-propelled grenades, AK-47 assault rifles, sniper rifles, 2.5 tons of explosives, and half a million rounds for various guns.

The weapons were manufactured in Iran and loaded onto the *Katrine A* at Kish Island, Iran. Many of the arms were still in factory wrappings, clearly marking them as having been produced in Iran.[15]

The shipment was part of Iran's ongoing mission to derail the Middle East peace talks by means of continuing violence.

THE GROWING NETWORK

Since September 11, 2001, Iran has made every effort to bring Muslim and Arab nations together against Israel and the United States. Syed Shahzad notes:

> The Iranian initiative seeks to persuade some of those countries that initially sided with the US into switching camps.... And these developments have brought many Arab and Middle Eastern nations closer together. Sources said that Iran played an important role in this and had been pursuing countries such as

Saudi Arabia and Kuwait in particular to help them restore their relations against Israel in the Middle East.... The test now will be how fast Arab and Muslim nations move to form a common stance, and how quickly the US takes measures to counter them.[16]

In a report titled "Patterns of Global Terrorism 2001," the U.S. State Department reported that Iran is "the most active state sponsor of terrorism."[17] Part of Iran's current threat against the U.S. and other Western nations is that it has a worldwide support network of terrorists who are ready and willing to launch attacks against U.S. interests.

THE SUM OF ALL FEARS

Of course, a nuclear Iran in and of itself is terrifying, but the worst fear is that Iran would pass these weapons to terrorists. If terrorists were to get their hands on these weapons, there is little doubt in anyone's mind that they would use them. Osama bin Laden has said, "Acquiring nuclear weapons for the defense of Moslems is a religious duty. If I have acquired these weapons, then I thank Allah for enabling me to do so."[18] He would thank Allah, and then he would unleash nuclear jihad against Israel and the U.S.

The results of this would be cataclysmic. Nicholas Kristof issued this sobering warning about the result of nuclear terror.

If a 10-kiloton terrorist nuclear weapon explodes beside the New York Stock Exchange or the U.S. Capitol or in Times Square, as many nuclear experts believe is likely in the next decade, then the next 9/11 commission will write a devastating critique of how we allowed that to happen. There is a general conviction among many experts—though, in fairness, not all—that nuclear terrorism has a better-than-even chance of occurring in the next 10 years. Such an attack could kill 500,000 people.[19]

Almost everyone has seen a picture of an atomic mushroom cloud, or film footage of an actual explosion. It's an unforgettable image that remains etched in our memory. However, in our world today, it's easy to forget the horror of nuclear weapons, though the threat is more real than at any time since 1945.

It's also possible Iran could pass this nuclear technology on to other radical Islamist states. In the spring of 2006, Ayatollah Ali Khamenei, the supreme leader of Iran, said his country is now ready to share its nuclear technology with neighboring states. Ayatollah Khamenei made the remarks in a meeting with the Sudanese president, Omar al-Bashir. During their meeting, Khamenei told President Bashir: "The Islamic Republic of Iran is prepared to transfer the experience, knowledge and technology of its scientists." Interestingly, Persia (Iran) and Cush (Sudan) are mentioned right next to one another in Ezekiel 38:5 as allies against Israel and the West in the end times. The growing relationship between Iran and Sudan is a signpost that points toward the fulfillment of Ezekiel 38–39.

RADICAL ISLAM AND TERROR

In a recent article, Andrew McCarthy has boldly noted what many have been afraid to say openly—that the current war on terror is really a war against radical Islam. The kind of radical Islam that is festering in Iran.

> Well, we are now well into the third year of what is called the 'War on Terror.' That is the language we all use, and it is ubiquitous. The tabloids and the more prestigious journals of news and opinion fill their pages with it. The 24-hour cable television stations are not content merely to repeat 'War on Terror' as if it were a mantra; they actually use it as a floating logo in their dizzying set designs. Most significant of all, the 'War on Terror' is our government's top rhetorical catch-phrase. It is the way we define for the American people and the world—especially the Islamic world—what we are doing, and what we are about. It is the way we explain the nature of the menace that we are striving to defeat. But is it accurate? Does it make sense? More importantly, does it serve our purposes? Does it make victory more identifiable, and hence more attainable? I humbly suggest that it fails on all these scores. This, furthermore, is no mere matter of rhetoric or semantics. It is all about substance, and it goes to the very core of our struggle.[20]

Then, McCarthy concludes with this politically incorrect, yet truthful, analysis.

> Terrorism is not an enemy. It is a method. It is the most sinister, brutal, inhumane method of our age. But it is nonetheless just that: a method. You cannot, and you do not, make war on a method. War is made on an identified—and identifiable—enemy. In the

here and now, that enemy is militant Islam—a very particular practice and interpretation of a very particular set of religious, political and social principles. Now that is a very disturbing, very discomfiting thing to say in 21st-century America. It is very judgmental. It sounds very insensitive. It is the very definition of politically incorrect. Saying it aloud will not get you invited to chat with Oprah. But it is a fact. And it is important both to say it and to understand it.[21]

I could not agree more. America and the world must realize that the greatest threat to the world today is militant Islam. The next great event in Bible prophecy could very well be the great Russian-Islamic invasion of Israel predicted in Ezekiel 38–39. It is a prophecy that is shaping history even as you read these words.

AN IMPORTANT DISCLAIMER

It's important for me to make a key disclaimer at this juncture. Since much of this book has to do with Iran, its new leader, and the Islamic religion, I want every reader to know that I do not hate followers of Islam. God loves people no matter what their particular ethnic background, errors, sins, or false beliefs might be. God is gracious and patient. He is never in a hurry to judge. But someday He will judge. And while there is still time we should do all we can to spread the gospel to Muslims in our own country and abroad.

I have visited Turkey and Jordan on several occasions on study and mission trips and have supported a Turkish pastor. I have a great burden to see the gospel of Christ reach people who have been misled by the teachings of Islam. My purpose is to simply state what I believe the Bible says about the final invasion of Israel by a Russian-Islamic alliance of nations.

Of course, the Bible never mentions Islam, since Islam was not founded until the seventh century AD and the New Testament was completed in AD 95. However, isn't it interesting that all the nations in Ezekiel 38:1–7 that attack Israel in the end times are currently Islamic nations with the exception of Russia? And most of them are currently avowed enemies of Israel (Persia, Libya, and Sudan). There is nothing that these nations would love more than to invade Israel to wipe her off the face of the earth. Obviously, God knew this when Ezekiel penned his prophecy in about 570 BC proving once again that the Bible is divine in origin.

SIGN OF THE TIMES

While what we see developing before our eyes in the world today is disturbing, it should not be surprising to those who understand Bible prophecy. It's an important sign of the times.

The rise of militant Islam is setting the stage for the end times in at least two key ways. First, it's contributing to world-wide instability and pushing the world toward globalism even faster than its already accelerating pace. Nations must come together in cooperative military and intelligence efforts to combat this terrible menace. And globalism is necessary for the worldwide rule of the Antichrist predicted in Revelation 13. Second, the meteoric rise of militant Islam is also setting the stage for the massive end-times invasion of Israel predicted by the Old Testament prophet Ezekiel 2,600 years ago.

The alliance of nations appears to be forming right before our eyes.

CHAPTER 5

IRAN'S PRESIDENT: THE NUCLEAR PROPHET

*Nuclear energy is our right, and we will resist
until this right is fully realized.*

MAHMOUD AHMADINEJAD, PRESIDENT OF THE
ISLAMIC REPUBLIC OF IRAN

In June 2005, Mahmoud Ahmadinejad was elected the sixth president of the Islamic Republic of Iran. He took office on August 3, 2005. Since that time, he has stirred up a firestorm of controversy with his bombastic, alarming statements about everything from nuclear weapons to Israel.

All the world seems to be asking—who is Mahmoud Ahmadinejad?

TERRORIST TIES

Ahmadinejad was born on October 28, 1956, and came from simple beginnings. He is the son of a blacksmith. He worked his way up the ladder, earning a PhD in engineering and serving as a member of the prestigious Revolutionary Guards.

There are still some serious, lingering questions about his alleged role in the Iran Hostage Crisis in 1979. Many believe that he was one of the leaders among the hostage-takers and that he personally conducted interrogations of American personnel during the 444-day hostage ordeal.[22]

Ahmadinejad was elected president in June 2005 on a Populist platform. He has a reputation for a simple life, and he campaigned against political corruption. He remains very popular among the core constituency of the revolution and government. He also enjoys the support of the Basij, which is a ten-million-strong militia that guards Islamic revolutionary values. Behind the smiling, Populist front is the heart of a revolutionary firebrand that has been smoldering since the days of the revolution.

SHOCKING STATEMENTS

When Mahmoud Ahmadinejad was elected president in June 2005, Jeffrey Gedmin of *The Weekly Standard* (7/9/05) issued this early warning.

> But no one doubts that a real...hard-liner, Mahmoud Ahmadinejad, has now been elected as Iran's new president. This should concentrate the mind. Ahmadinejad calls himself a fundamentalist. He was an officer of the Islamic Revolutionary Guard, taught for years at the Revolutionary Guard's staff college, and has served as special emissary for the 'Supreme Guide' on a number of domestic and foreign policy missions. He supported the fatwa against author Salman Rushdie, of course, and by all accounts Ahmadinejad is a real-deal Islamist.

However, few were prepared for what was coming.

On June 30, 2005, his initial statement in Tehran as president-elect was an announcement that the government was going back to its brutal beginnings. "Thanks be to the blood of the martyrs, a new Islamic revolution has arisen and the Islamic revolution of 1384 [the current Iranian year] will, if God wills, cut off the roots of injustice in the world. The era of oppression, hegemonic regimes, tyranny, and injustice has reached its end.... The wave of the Islamic revolution will soon reach the entire world."[23]

Since that time, in just a year in office, Ahmadinejad has been a propaganda machine for radical Islam and Iran's hardline. Here is just a small sample of the kinds of statements he regularly makes.

"We did not have a revolution in order to have democracy."

"If anyone shows aggression to the Iranian nation's rights, Iran will wipe the dark stain of regret on their foreheads."

"If the world accepts Iran's desire then fine, but if it wants to ignore the rights of the Iranian nation then Iran will know what path to pursue."

"If we stand strong the enemies will be defeated in the face of the Iranian nation's will."

"Today the Iranian nation is standing firm against the world's bullies and oppressors, and the people will not back down even one step from its right in seeking nuclear technology."

"We are in the process of an historical war between the World of Arrogance [i.e., the West] and the Islamic world."

"The Iranian nation will resist with God's help."

Ahmadinejad has threatened to "cut off the hands of any aggressor" if Iran is attacked.

He has threatened to unleash 40,000 volunteer homicide bombers against U.S. interests and any nations that cooperate with the U.S. if it hits Iran's nuclear facilities.

At a rally in February 2006 celebrating the anniversary of the 1979 Islamic Revolution, Ahmadinejad said, "Nuclear energy is our right, and we will resist until this right is fully realized." The crowd responded in unison with the chant, "Nuclear energy is our inalienable right." Ahmadinejad called on the people to prepare for what's ahead when he said, "I ask our dear people to prepare themselves for a great struggle."

To mark the start of the Iranian year, on March 21, 2006, he said, "No one can take away our nuclear technology. The Iranian nation has obtained it and will preserve it. Some are against the Iranian nation's development."

Ahmadinejad has a steely determination to get his hands on nuclear weapons.

VIRULENT ANTI-SEMITE

Ahmadinejad's rhetoric about nuclear weapons is certainly troubling, but his most venomous statements have been directed toward Israel and the Jewish people. On October 26, 2005, at a conference titled "A World Without Zionism," Ahmadinejad addressed a gathering of about 4,000 students. Standing in front of a huge banner that read, "A World Without Zionism," he dropped several verbal bombshells: "They [ask], 'Is it possible for us to witness a world without America and Zionism?' But you had best know that this slogan and this goal are altogether attainable, and surely can be achieved. This regime that is occupying Jerusalem must be wiped from the map."

The only bit of good news for Israel in these statements is that at least Ahmadinejad has recognized that Israel is on the map. No Arab or Islamic nation up to this point has even recognized the existence of the Jewish state or included Israel on any map of the region. Also, it's important to note that Ahmadinejad was simply quoting what the Ayatollah Khomeini had already said years earlier. The idea of wiping Israel off the map is nothing new for Iran, but it was the first time that the rest of the world was introduced to Iran's real agenda.

Ahmadinejad has made a number of other aggressive, inflammatory, anti-Semitic statements.

"No doubt the new wave (of attacks) in Palestine will soon wipe off this disgraceful blot (Israel) from the face of the Islamic world."

"The establishment of the Zionist regime was a move by the world oppressor against the Islamic world."

"Palestine is the center of the final stages of the battle between Islam and arrogance."

"The skirmishes in the occupied land are part of a war of destiny. The outcome of hundreds of years of war will be defined in Palestinian land."

"We should not settle for a piece of land."

"Some 60 years have passed since the end of World War II. Why should the people of Germany and Palestine pay now for a war in which the current generation was not involved?"

"The Islamic *umma* (community) will not allow its historic enemy to live in its heartland."

"Anyone who signs a treaty with Israel means he has signed the surrender of the Muslim world."

"We say that this fake regime (Israel) cannot logically continue to live."

At the Tehran Conference Ahmadinejad said, "Whether you like it or not, the Zionist regime is on the road to being eliminated."

On December 8, 2005, he said that Israel should be moved to Europe and questioned whether the Jewish Holocaust ever occurred. In further remarks, President Ahmadinejad implied that European countries backed the formation of Israel in the Middle East in 1948 primarily out of guilt over the Nazi genocide. He said, "Some European countries insist on saying that during World War II, Hitler burned millions of Jews and put them in concentration camps." He also said, "Any historian, commentator or scientist who doubts that is taken to prison or gets condemned. Let's assume what the Europeans say is true.... Let's give some land to the Zionists in Europe or in Germany or Austria. They faced injustice in Europe, so why do the repercussions fall on the Palestinians?"

These statements have met with universal condemnation by the West, but the nations of the Middle East have been strangely silent. And their silence is certainly indicative of their approval of his venomous anti-Semitism.

Ahmadinejad's anti-Semitism has blinded him to such an extent that he even went so far as to blame Israel and the U.S. for the bombing of a Shiite shrine in Iraq on February 22, 2006, by rival Sunnis. The *Daily News* issued this report.

Iran's President Mahmoud Ahmadinejad yesterday warned Western powers like the US and Israel that they would face the wrath of Muslims following the devastating bombing of a Shi'ite shrine in Iraq. Echoing Supreme leader Ayatollah Ali Khamenei, Ahmadinejad pinned the blame for Wednesday's Samarra shrine bombing on 'Zionists' and foreign forces in Iraq. 'These heinous acts are committed by a group of Zionists and occupiers that have failed. They have failed in the face of Islam's logic and justice,' Ahmadinejad said in a speech broadcast live on state television. 'But be sure, you will not be saved from the wrath and power of the justice-seeking nations by resorting to such acts,' he said to cries of 'Death to America' 'Death to Israel' from a crowd of thousands of supporters in central Iran.[24]

In the same vein as Hitler in his infamous *Mein Kampf*, Iran's leader has given the world every reason to believe, that if given the opportunity, he wouldn't hesitate to commit genocide. In his mind every problem in the world can be laid at Israel's doorstep. Israel's acting Prime Minister, Ehud Olmert, has accurately accused Iran's President of being "obsessed with anti-Semitic hatred."

THE DAMASCUS DUO

After some of his most inflammatory statements about Israel and nuclear weapons, Ahmadinejad sought refuge in the embrace of a friend, so he immediately visited Syrian President Bahar al-Assad. Syria stands with Iran as a state-sponsor of terror and hater of Israel.

At a joint news conference in January 2005, Assad said, "We support the right of Iran and any state in the world to acquire peaceful technology."

These two nations, who both face increasing international pressure and the threat of a United Nations showdown, are regional terror allies. Together Ahmadinejad and Assad are a menace to the Middle East and the world. Iran's growing ties with Syria under Ahmadinejad are another twist in the downward spiral. Israel has warned that Iran, Syria, and the Hamas-run Palestinian government form an "axis of terror" that is sowing the seeds of the first world war of the 21st century. This prediction may not be far off the mark.

THE MYSTICAL MENACE

It would be terrifying enough if this were the whole story about Iran's new president, but there's one more angle to the headlines from Iran that should send a shiver down the spine of every person on earth. There's a fanatical, superstitious, religious dimension to this entire picture.

Iran's new president is motivated by an apocalyptic, end-of-days Messianism that many fear is giving him a dangerous sense of divine destiny. He believes the apocalypse will occur in his own lifetime, and he's not even fifty years old. Many of his statements suggest that he believes his reign is destined to bring about the end times. This is quite a vision for a mere mortal.

Ahmadinejad is a Shiite Muslim who is deeply committed to an Islamic Messianic figure known as the Mahdi (Arabic for "rightly-guided one") or sometimes referred to as the Hidden Imam. He has a presidential obsession with what is known in Islam as Mahdaviat. This is a technical religious term that means "a belief in and efforts to prepare for the Mahdi."

As mayor of Tehran, Ahmadinejad persuaded the city council to build a grand avenue in the city to prepare for the coming of the *Mahdi*, the key figure in Islamic eschatology. When he came to power as president, one of the initial acts of his government was to donate $17 million to the Jamkaran mosque, which is a popular pilgrimage site where Muslim devotees come to drop messages in a well where they believe the Hidden Imam is hiding.

Ahmadinejad is a self-proclaimed apostle on a misguided mission from Allah.

Anton La Guardia makes this chilling observation about Ahmadinejad's "Apocalypse Now" theology:

All streams of Islam believe in a divine saviour, known as the Mahdi, who will appear at the End of Days. A common rumour—denied by the government but widely believed—is that Mr. Ahmadinejad and his cabinet have signed a 'contract' pledging themselves to work for the return of the Mahdi and sent it to Jamkaran. Iran's dominant 'Twelver' sect believes this will be Mohammed ibn Hasan, regarded as the 12th Imam, or righteous descendant of the Prophet Mohammad. He is said to have gone into 'occlusion' in the ninth century, at the age of five. His return will be preceded by cosmic chaos, war and bloodshed. After a cataclysmic confrontation with evil and darkness, the Mahdi will lead the world to an era of universal peace. This is similar to the Christian vision of the Apocalypse. Indeed, the Hidden Imam is expected to return in the company of Jesus. Mr Ahmadinejad appears to believe that these events are close at hand and that ordinary mortals can influence the divine timetable. The prospect of such a man obtaining nuclear weapons is worrying. The unspoken question is this: is Mr. Ahmadinejad now tempting a clash with the West because he feels safe in the belief of the imminent

return of the Hidden Imam? Worse, might he be trying to provoke chaos in the hope of hastening his
reappearance?[25]

Within Shiite Islam, which dominates Iran, an Imam is a
spiritual leader who is allegedly a bloodline relative of the
prophet Muhammad. There is a prophecy in Islam about the
coming of the twelfth Imam—Imam Muhammad Abul
Qasim. It's believed by the Twelver sect that he disappeared in
AD 878 in the cave of the great mosque of Samarra without
leaving any descendants. It's also taught that the twelfth Imam
was still active and communicated with the outside world by
messengers until AD 941 when all communication and con-
tact with this world was cut off.

According to Islamic teaching, he will return near the end
of the world. According to their end-time view, when he
returns, he will rule the earth for seven years, bringing about
the Final Judgment and end of the world.[26] The mention of a
seven-year rule for the Mahdi is interesting to me because the
Bible predicts that the Antichrist or false messiah will hold
sway over the earth for seven years, ruling the entire world for
the final half of the seven-year period. Could it be that the
Islamic expectation of a messiah who will rule for seven years
could set them up to initially accept such a leader who will
make a seven-year peace treaty according to Daniel 9:27?

In any event, Ahmadinejad's politics cannot be divorced
from his fundamental religious views about the Hidden Imam.
He believes in the prophetic outline of the Twelfth Imam and
believes that he is to do all he can to bring about its fulfillment.
He has reportedly said that he believes the return of the Imam
is only two years away.

THE SECRET SOCIETY

To make matters even worse, if that's possible, Ahmadinejad is close to the messianic Hojatieh society that is led by Ayatollah Mesbah Yazdi. This spiritual leader frequently appears with the new president in public. The Hojatieh believe that only great tribulation, increased violence, and conflict will bring about his coming. They believe that the "creation of chaos on earth" can accelerate the Imam's return. Ahmadinejad believes that the Mahdi will appear when the globe is in utter chaos. This kind of end-of-days theology is what drives and compels Ahmadinejad.

For Ahmadinejad, a war with the West would be a kind of "welcome mat" for the Mahdi.

His apocalyptic view is so strongly ingrained that he has fired all of Iran's most experienced diplomats and many other officials who don't share his view of the coming apocalyptic conflagration and has replaced many of them with fellow zealots.[27] In his bestselling book, *Countdown to Crisis*, Kenneth Timmerman notes: "Since taking the reins of government in August, Ahmadinejad has placed Hojatieh devotees in his cabinet and throughout the bureaucracy. The Ministry of Information and Security (MOIS), largely sidelined by reformers under President Khatami, had re-emerged as a powerful repressive force, using plainclothes security agents, allied with parliamentary Basij and non-government vigilantes, to crack down on potential opponents of the regime."

VISIONS OF GRANDEUR

On November 16, 2005, in a speech in Tehran to senior clerics, Ahmadinejad said that the primary mission of his regime was to "pave the path for the glorious reappearance of the

Imam Mahdi (May God Hasten His Reappearance)."[28] His sense of destiny seems clear in his own mind.

Ahmadinejad delivered a speech at the United Nations in September 2005, not long after he assumed the presidency, that many onlookers were expecting would be conciliatory. However, he spoke in apocalyptic terms and ended the speech with a messianic appeal to God to "hasten the emergence of your last repository, the Promised One, that perfect and pure human being, the one that will fill this world with justice and peace."

Anton La Guardia gave this report about the UN speech.

In a video distributed by an Iranian website in November Mr. Ahmadinejad described how one of his colleagues had claimed to have seen a glow of light around him as he began his speech. 'I felt it myself too,' Mr. Ahmadinejad recounts. 'I felt that all of a sudden the atmosphere changed there. And for 27–28 minutes all the leaders did not blink... It's not an exaggeration, because I was looking.' Western officials said the real reason for any open-eyed stares from delegates was that 'they couldn't believe what they were hearing from Ahmadinejad.' Their sneaking suspicion is that he relishes a clash with the West in the conviction that it would rekindle the spirit of the Islamic revolution and speed up the arrival of the Hidden Imam.[29]

Daniel Pipes highlights Ahmadinejad's own account of the UN address and his otherworldly experience.

One of our group told me that when I started to say 'In the name of God the almighty and merciful,' he saw a light around me, and I was placed inside this aura. I felt it myself. I felt the atmosphere suddenly change, and for those 27 or 28 minutes, the leaders of the world did not blink. … And they were rapt. It seemed as if a hand was holding them there and had opened their eyes to receive the message from the Islamic republic."[30]

Talk about eery! This sounds Satanic. It's reminiscent of Hitler's mesmerizing speeches to the German people. German chancellor Angela Merkel has openly compared the Iranian President to Adolf Hitler.

Iran's new president is one who will not hesitate to pull the trigger to bring his view of the apocalypse to fruition.

Mortimer Zuckerman sounds this warning.

"Iran today is in the grip of yet a new wave of extremists. Its president, Mahmoud Ahmadinejad, is a revolutionary firebrand who has directly threatened the West. In his own words, 'We are in the process of an historical war between the World of Arrogance [i.e., the West] and the Islamic world.' His foreign policy ambition is an Islamic government for the whole world, under the leadership of the Mahdi, the absent imam of the Shiites—code language for the export of radical Islam. And he casts himself as Hitler reincarnated, calling for Israel to be "wiped off the map." Who can think that Iran poses no threat to world peace? History tells us that when madmen call for genocide, they usually mean it."[31]

In light of the current situation, the invasion of Israel by Iran and her allies, predicted by the prophet Ezekiel, may not be far away!

CHAPTER 6

FACING A NUCLEAR IRAN

If Iran is allowed to produce nuclear weapons,
the genie will be out of the bottle,
and the whole world will be in grave danger.
HENRY KISSINGER

They're progressing much faster than we thought they would.
They seem to know what they're doing.
U.S. OFFICIAL

I live in Edmond, Oklahoma, which is just north and east of Oklahoma City, but I grew up in Oklahoma City. One of the unique features about Oklahoma City it that it's the crossroads of the nation. About ten miles south of my house the two great arteries of our nation intersect—I-35 and I-40. This convergence point lies in the very heart of our nation. Millions of tons of the things we eat, use, and consume pass this critical crossroads each year.

Iran today is at the crossroads of the world's crisis. Two key highways are intersecting there that may affect the life of every person on earth. What are they? The perilous crossroad of radical Islam and nuclear technology (and if you want to add a third highway, it would be oil). The convergence of these two factors in the same place at the same time is the world's gravest danger.

The reality of terrorists, or apocalyticists like Mahmoud Ahmadinejad, with nuclear weapons is too terrible to fathom. Yet, to our dismay, one of these highways is already in place, and the other one may not be lagging far behind. Iran is working feverishly and clandestinely to get the bomb. While the world continues to talk, Iran continues to build. Iran has recently allotted $213 million for construction of nuclear facilities. Satellites have revealed that Iran has built a new tunnel entrance at Isfahan, where uranium is processed into a feed material for enrichment. It has also reinforced its Natanz underground uranium enrichment plant to further secure it against any attack. Iran knows that if it keeps negotiating long enough it can easily capitalize on the overextension of the U.S. military and the West's reluctance to escalate the matter any further. This "talk and build" strategy is working and will continue to buy precious time for Iran to join the nuclear club.

To better understand the severity of the threat posed by Iran, we need a brief overview of exactly what Iran has been up to. To put it shortly, Iran now has multiple sites in its nuclear megaplex ranging from mining to production.

Here's a brief flyover of Iran's nuclear program:

IRAN'S NUCLEAR MEGAPLEX

MINING: Saghand. Uranium ore mining begins later this year with expected annual yield of 50–60 tons.

MILLING: Ardkan. Uranium ore to yellowcake (uranium ore concentrate).

MILLING: Gehine. Mining and milling to produce yellowcake.

CONVERSION: Isfahan. Yellowcake becomes hexafluoride (UF6) or hex, ready for enrichment.

ENRICHMENT: Natanz. Iran's largest nuclear facility, housing thousands of centrifuges capable of processing weapons-grade uranium.

PRODUCTION: Arak. Heavy-water reactor suited for weapons-grade plutonium production.

PRODUCTION: Bushehr. Russian-built light water reactor due for start-up this year for reactor-grade plutonium.

PRODUCTION: Khuzestan. New reactor planned.[32]

IRAN'S EIGHT NUCLEAR FACILITIES

Bonab

Bonab Atomic Energy Research Center conducts research on food irradiation and other agricultural issues.

Bushehr

Two partially completed reactors. Bushehr #1 is being completed with Russian assistance. The status of the spent nuclear fuel is an open question.

Fasa

This facility is thought to be the site of a uranium hexafluoride gas conversion plant, or some other form of nuclear research center.

Tehran

Sharif University of Technology is Iran's central repository for nuclear research. It is also the alleged site of their uranium centrifuge research. There are two small research reactors at the University of Tehran.

Ardekan

Possible uranium conversion facility to convert uranium ore to nuclear fuel for use in the Bushehr reactor.

Natanz

Uranium enrichment facility. During inspections in 2003, IAEA inspectors found particles of highly enriched uranium (HEU). Iran claimed the contamination was from the supplier country, which has not been named.

Khusab

Plutonium production reactor under construction. If completed, in conjunction with the plutonium extraction plants, it could create a significant inventory of un-safeguarded, weapons-usable plutonium.

Isfahan

Iran's largest nuclear research center. About 3,000 scientists work here. There is a small research reactor on site, and plans for a larger reactor and uranium enrichment facilities have been acknowledged.[33]

PREPARING FOR BATTLE

Iran keeps issuing bold threats and is making preparations for whatever lies ahead. The Iranian government claims that it's ready for any U.S. or Israeli attempt to take out its nuclear program. General Yahya Rahim Safavi, the head of the Iranian Revolutionary Guards said, "You can start a war but it won't be you who finishes it. We have American forces in the region under total surveillance. For the past two years, we have been ready for any scenario, whether sanctions or an attack."

Iran's military has reported that it successfully test-fired a missile that can employ multiple warheads, hit several targets simultaneously, and is not detectable by radar. It's called the Fajr-3 missile, which means "victory" in the Farsi language. The missile can reach Israel and U.S. military bases in the Middle East. It's not yet known if this missile could be armed with a nuclear warhead.

Iranian officials have also confidently stated that military strikes against Iran's nuclear sites would not destroy the Islamic republic's uranium enrichment activities since they could be easily moved and restarted. Aliasghar Soltaniyeh, Iran's ambassador to the International Atomic Energy Agency in Vienna said, "You know very well...we can enrich uranium anywhere in the country, with a vast country of more than 1 million 600 square kilometers. Enrichment can be done anywhere in Iran."[34]

It sounds like Iran is prepared and that it will require ground and air attacks to fully dismantle their nuclear program. However, Iran has about three times the population of Iraq and four times the geographic area. Its mountain ranges represent formidable barriers to conventional warfare. Successfully taking out Iran's nuclear facilities is a daunting task.

THE POLLS ARE NOT PROMISING

One of the outside hopes for Western nations is that the radical government of Mahmoud Ahmedinejad might be overthrown from within. Many experts are encouraging the U.S. government to take every measure to spark regime change in Iran.

While there is certainly some unrest in Iran over economic issues and government repression, the idea of getting a nuclear weapon is popular with the Iranian people, even those who don't favor the present regime. An opinion poll in early 2006 in the government-run Iranian newspaper claims that 74.3 percent of Iranians surveyed favor the policy of pursuing a nuclear program. While it's very possible that this poll is sheer propaganda, if it's even close to reality, this does not bode well for a moderate uprising in Iran anytime soon.

Moreover, as noted earlier, Ahmadinejad presently enjoys support from the core constituency of the revolution and the government, as well as the ten-million member Basij, which is a militia that guards Islamic revolutionary values. At this time regime change doesn't look very promising.

THE EZEKIEL PROPHECY

Writing 2,600 years ago, the Jewish prophet Ezekiel predicted that a coalition of nations from every point on the compass would converge on Israel to destroy her. That ancient prophecy foretells Iran's place in the end times and specifically names Iran's allies.

According to Ezekiel's prophecy, one of Iran's allies in the end times will be the great Russian bear. And currently, the ties between Iran and Russia are growing closer every day.

Join me now as we track the bear in Ezekiel 38–39. We'll find that her footprints lead right to the land of Israel.

CHAPTER 7

THE IRANIAN-RUSSIAN CONNECTION

Russia is back.
ALEXEI MALASHENKO

Two of the ancient place-names in Ezekiel's great end-time prophecy in Ezekiel 38–39 are Rosh and Persia. There's no doubt that Persia is the ancient counterpart to modern Iran. The name was changed in 1935. As we will see in more detail in chapter 12, ancient Rosh is the modern nation of Russia.

THE RISE OF RUSSIA

The rise of Russia in the last century to a place of world prominence is no accident. It's a key piece of furniture on the end-time stage that must be in place for the final drama to unfold.

Many falsely believed that when the Soviet Union came apart that a Russian-led invasion of Israel seemed very unlikely. However, Russia today shows every sign of going back to her totalitarian days and back to her Islamic allies—especially Iran.

It's fascinating that these two nations, Russia and Iran, which are growing closer together even as you read this, are mentioned as allies in the end times in a prophecy written about 2,600 years ago.

RUSSIA'S MIDDLE EAST MOVE

In the last few years, Russia has begun to reassert and resurrect her influence in the Middle East. There's a growing alliance between Russia and Muslim nations. Russian President Vladimir Putin clearly aims to reestablish Russian clout in the Middle East to at least challenge, if not replace, Western-dominated diplomacy. Russia is developing strong relations with Syria, Iran, and the Palestinians. Right after the Palestinian elections in which the Islamic terrorist organization Hamas garnered the most votes, Russian President Putin invited Hamas to visit Russia. Putin said that he never considered Hamas to be a terrorist organization.

Russia's reassertion up to this point has primarily been in the form of weapon's sales. Between 1989 and 1993 Iran purchased $10 billion of weapons from Russia, and also began to buy Russian nuclear and ballistic missile technology. In 1992, Iran signed an agreement with Russia to revitalize their nuclear reactors that had been damaged in the war with Iraq. The agreement called for Russia to supply Iran with two 440-megawatt reactors. Russia is helping Iran build its first nuclear power plant at Bushehr. It is estimated that Iran will be able to assemble nuclear weapons in five years, but possibly much sooner. In March 2001, Iran's President Mohammad Khatami visited Russia to forge stronger ties between the two nations. After the meeting, Russian president Vladimir Putin said that Russia would resume sales of conventional arms to Iran and help Iran complete its nuclear reactor near Bushehr.

For several years, Russia and Iran have been establishing and strengthening their ties. Specifically, Russia has been the chief source of Iranian weapons purchasing and development.

In November 2005, Russia and Iran signed an arms deal worth $1 billion. Russia agreed to sell thirty TOR-M1 surface-to-air missiles and other defense systems to Iran over the next two years. The TOR-M1 missile system is the most advanced system available. It can identify up to 48 targets and fire at two targets simultaneously at an altitude of up to 20,000 feet. At the same time, Russia and Iran also reached a deal on modernizing Iran's air force inventory.

Until recently, most of Russia's help has been in the form of conventional weaponry, but that seems to be changing. And in a hurry.

Associated Press reporter Ali Akbar Dareini filed this report on August 23, 2004.

Iran said yesterday that it plans to build a second nuclear reactor with Russia's help and that at least two other European states have expressed interest in such a project, brushing aside US accusations that the Islamic state wants to build atomic weapons. Russia is building Iran's first nuclear reactor, which was begun by West Germany but interrupted during the 1979 Islamic revolution. Damage caused to the nearly completed facility in Bushehr during Iran's 1980–88 war with Iraq also led to the postponement of its planned inauguration from 2003 to August 2006. Despite the delays and the project's $800 million cost, Iranian nuclear officials say they want Russia to build more nuclear reactors to help generate greater amounts of electricity. The comments yesterday reflect Iran's determination to push ahead with its nuclear program despite US and international concerns that it seeks to develop nuclear weapons. The

United States has been lobbying for the International Atomic Energy Agency to refer Iran's nuclear dossier to the Security Council. Tehran denies seeking to develop weapons. Asadollah Sabouri, deputy head of the Atomic Energy Organization of Iran, did not say when construction might begin but insisted Russia was obligated to build more than one nuclear reactor under a 1992 agreement between the two countries. 'We have contracts with Russia to build more nuclear reactors. No number has been specified but definitely our contract with Russia is to build more than one nuclear power plant,' Sabouri said, adding that Tehran has carried out several studies and technical reports for the construction of new facilities.

But Russia's military sales are not limited to Iran. In March 2006, Russia agreed to sell 7.5 billion dollars worth of weapons and combat planes to Algeria—an Islamic nation in North Africa. As part of the deal, Russia agreed to write off 4.7 billion dollars of Algerian debt from the Soviet era. This huge arms deal is seen as another indicator that Russia is determined to become a significant player in the Middle East.

URANIUM OFFER

Russian ties with Iran have further deepened as Russia has repeatedly offered to help Iran with its uranium enrichment in an effort to quell international unrest over Iran's nuclear program. Russia's offer is really the only negotiating tool or compromise plan that has been available to try to deter Iran's nuclear ambitions.

The gist of the offer is that Iran could deliver its uranium to Russia where it would be enriched and then sent back to Iran for peaceful use. Russian enrichment of Iran's uranium would allegedly give the world much more peace of mind about Iran's intentions.

While there is little hope that this solution would ever satisfy either Iran or the West, Russia's offer is another example of Russia's expanding role and influence in the Middle East and in Iran. Russia appears determined to woo the Islamic world with guns and offers of diplomacy.

RUSSIAN APPEASEMENT

Russia, which has a strategic vote on the UN Security Council, is also helping Iran out on the diplomatic front. While publicly urging Iran not to enrich uranium, Russia consistently refuses to even entertain the possibility of any meaningful consequences for Iran if it keeps pursuing its present course. Of course, everyone wants to see the Iran crisis solved peacefully, but Russia's position is nothing short of appeasement. As the United States and Europe push for the threat of sanctions and even military force as a final option, Russia has carefully avoided anything that even looks like a threat. Russia has even warned the West that threats will only "aggravate the international standoff over Tehran's suspect nuclear program."[35] The current crisis is exposing Russia's close ties with Iran for the world to see. This is further evidence of their growing alliance.[35]

BACK TO THE U.S.S.R.

At the same time Russia is resurrecting its influence and support of Iran and the rest of the Muslim world, it's also on a fast-track back to its old totalitarian ways.

On April 25, 2005, Russian President Vladimir Putin delivered his annual state of the nation speech to lawmakers at the Kremlin. The speech to the Russian Parliament, which lasted 50 minutes, mourned the fall of the Soviet Union. The Russians, who are awash in nostalgia, have called WWII the "Great Patriotic War."

In his own nostalgic moment, Putin made it clear that he would greatly prefer the Soviet empire to the modern state of Russia. Putin served as a colonel in the KGB, and there have been rising fears that he is reversing many of the democratic advances in Russia. Many of his actions point to the fact that he would prefer a return to the "good ol' days" of the Soviet empire. He has resurrected some communist symbols during his presidency such as bringing back "the music of the old Soviet-anthem and the Soviet-style red banner as the military's flag."[36]

President Bush raised the issue of Putin's commitment to democracy in a meeting in Slovakia in February 2006. There are rising fears that Putin could lead Russia back to her days as head of the communist empire.

In his annual address, Putin described the fall of the Soviet Union like this. "First and foremost, it is worth acknowledging that the demise of the Soviet Union was the greatest geopolitical catastrophe of the century. As for the Russian people, it became a genuine tragedy. Tens of millions of our fellow citizens and countrymen found themselves beyond the fringes of Russian territory. The epidemic of collapse has spilled over to

Russia itself." This sounds like a man who would love to see Russia return to her glory days.

When the Soviet Union came apart in 1991, many believed that the Russian bear would go into permanent hibernation. For a while things in Russia looked promising. But recently, flush with huge oil and gas revenues, President Putin has taken advantage of his popularity to move Russia back toward dictatorship. Putin and all of his top advisors are former KGB members.

In his National Security Strategy in 2006, President Bush said that in Russia, "Recent trends regrettably point toward a diminishing commitment to democratic freedoms and institutions... Efforts to prevent democratic development at home or abroad will hamper the development of Russia's relations with the United States, Europe and its neighbors."

Watching Russia move back to the days of autocracy and at the same time cozy up to Iran and other Muslim nations fits the prophecy of Ezekiel 38–39 to a tee.

HOOKS IN THE JAWS

Mortimer B. Zuckerman, in a *U.S. News and World Report* article from January 30, 2006, says that "Russia today has become part of the problem, not the solution.... And Russia has made the threat more real. It sold the nuclear power plant at Bushehr to Iran and contracted to sell even more to bring cash into its nuclear industry."

Then Zuckerman noted that one American diplomat said that Russia's business with Iran is a "giant hook in Russia's jaw." What? Let me repeat that. The American diplomat said, "this business is a 'giant hook in Russia's jaw.'" That's right. The diplomat used a key phrase right out of Ezekiel 38 to describe Russia's current relationship with Iran.

Ezekiel 38:4, speaking to the last-days leader of Russia, says, "And I will turn you about, and *put hooks in your jaws*, and I will bring you out, and all your army, horses and horsemen, all of them splendidly attired, a great company with buckler and shield, all of them wielding swords."

It's very possible that something like the scenario we see today could be the "hooks in the jaw" that God uses to pull a reluctant Russia down into the land of Israel in the latter years. Russia's geopolitical strategy to deepen its relationship with Iran and other Muslim nations could very well be what will pull them into Israel in the end times as Ezekiel predicted.

Prophecy expert Thomas Ice envisions this kind of future scenario:

> I could see the Muslims coming to the Russians and telling them that America has set a precedent for an outside power coming into the Middle East to right a perceived wrong. (America has done it again in recent years by going into Afghanistan and Iraq.) On that basis, Russia should help out her Muslim friends by leading them in an overwhelming invasion of Israel in order to solve the Middle East Conflict in favor of the Islamic nations. Will this be the 'hook in the jaw' of Gog? Only time will tell. But something is up in the Middle East and Russia appears to have her fingerprints all over things. We know that the Bible predicts just such an alignment and invasion to take place 'in the latter years.'[37]

I wholeheartedly agree. And Russia's developing ties with Iran and other Muslim nations could very well be the setting of the hook.

CHAPTER 8

OIL: IRAN'S X-FACTOR

Sometime in 2006, mankind's thirst for oil will have crossed the milestone of 86 million barrels per day, which translates to a staggering one thousand barrels a second! Picture an Olympic-sized swimming pool full of oil: we would drain it in about 15 seconds. In one day, we empty close to 5500 such swimming pools. There are 192 countries in the world, and nearly all are dependent on oil. On the flip side, only 30 countries produce oil of any significant quantity, and only 17 of them are exporters of oil greater than 500,000 barrels a day. Geography and politics limit choice.

PETER TERTZAKIAN, *A THOUSAND BARRELS A SECOND*

The picture for long-term oil is not encouraging.

PAUL ROBERTS, *THE END OF OIL*

It seems clear from the Bible that in the end times the Middle East will be the number one crisis in the world. It will be center stage. The coming world ruler will burst on the world scene by making some kind of peace treaty with Israel, probably solving, albeit temporarily, the Middle East crisis.

This same ruler will apparently build an economic headquarters in Babylon, which is in modern Iraq (Revelation 17–18). And then, according to Revelation 16, all the nations of the earth will ultimately convene in northern Israel at Armageddon.

Years ago, students of Bible prophecy wondered what could possibly move the Middle East to the center of the world stage. But now we know.

There's the protracted, agonizing Israeli-Palestinian stand-off. There's the rise of radical Islam and the wave of terror that's sweeping the earth. And of course, in this same area, one can find about two-thirds of the world's proven oil reserves that keep the world's economy humming. Israel, terror, and oil have converged simultaneously to shine the world spotlight on the Middle East in a way no one could have imagined even fifty years ago.

While all of the Middle East is embroiled in these issues, Iran is in the center of the spotlight right now because of her sponsorship of terror, pursuit of nuclear weapons, and the sometimes forgotten oil factor.

THE WORLD'S OIL LIFELINE

The margin between oil supply and demand today is razor thin. At present, we are basically pumping out crude oil at about the same rate we're consuming it—1,000 barrels a second.[38] The level of spare capacity (known as the world's safety blanket) is only about two million barrels a day. This means that the world's oil supply chains are operating at an unbelievable 97.5 percent capacity. This leaves almost no margin for error for such things as natural disasters, accidents, terrorist attacks, geopolitical stress, or whatever else could disrupt the fragile supply chain.

Not long ago, in February 2004, oil was under $33 a barrel. Today it's at least double that, with no signs of letting up. As the U.S. continues to consume more and more oil, China's booming economy is just beginning to make its impact on world oil markets. World demand shows no signs of slowing, while supply and production remain static. Refineries today have no cushion. Refining capacity is currently at 96 percent, and no new refinery has been built in the U.S. since 1976.

We are all painfully aware that oil prices rise or fall on the slightest threat of disruption in supply. The day after Hurricane Katrina hit the U.S. Gulf Coast, the price of a gallon of gas shot up thirty cents overnight at the pump. Driving south on I-35, I saw something that I never dreamed I would see in my lifetime—a sign at a gas station advertising a gallon of gas for...$3.00. Just think what will happen to the U.S. economy when the price of a gallon of gas in the U.S. hits and stays at $3.00, $4.00, or even $5.00 a gallon. Or if there's some act of terror or natural disaster that shuts down the oil supply for an extended period of time. Pandemonium will erupt. Nations will begin to hoard oil. Individuals will try to hoard. Long lines at the gas pump will be commonplace. People won't be able to heat their homes.

Unfortunately, the situation doesn't look like it will improve anytime soon, if ever. As Peter Tertzakian notes, "Because big economies like the United States, China, and whole host of industrializing countries still have a positively correlated relationship between GDP and oil demand, the world as a whole requires an increasing amount of oil every year to facilitate economic growth. This is a crucial point, because pressure on the world's oil supply chains will keep building so long as the global economy keeps expanding. Any global economic growth at all necessitates more and more oil every year."[39]

Demand continues to escalate at an alarming rate. Here's a

brief survey of daily world oil consumption over the last five years.

2002   79 million barrels a day

2003   82.5 million barrels a day

2004   84.5 million barrels a day

2005   85 million barrels a day

2006   86 million barrels a day (estimated)[40]

By 2010, world consumption may hit 95 million barrels a day.[41] As demand continues to rise, and the oil supply lifeline becomes more fragile and vulnerable, disaster looms.

OVER A BARREL

Let's face it. The world runs on oil. And while the world is not running out of oil, the oil we need is getting harder to find. To put it another way, the world isn't running out of oil, but it is running out of cheap oil. Shallow reserves are getting much harder to find; therefore, the oil of the future will be much more expensive. And, at the same time, America is using more and more oil.

In 1985 the U.S. imported less than 30 percent of its oil. By 1990 the U.S. was importing almost 50 percent of its needed oil. At the current rate of unimpeded growth in oil imports, by 2015 America will be 70–75 percent dependent on foreign oil.

Addressing the issue of the coming peak in world oil production, *National Geographic* reports: "It could be 5 years from now or 30: No one knows for sure, and geologists and economists are embroiled in debate about just when the 'oil peak' will be upon us. But few doubt that it is coming. 'In our lifetime,' says economist Robert K. Kaufmann of Boston

University, who is 46, 'we will have to deal with a peak in the supply of cheap oil.' The peak will be a watershed moment, making the change from an increasing supply of cheap oil to a dwindling supply of expensive oil."[42]

Some experts think the worldwide oil production peak will occur in 2016, but that outside the Middle East it will occur in 2006. Others believe the peak outside the Middle East is already here.[43] This is especially troubling when one considers that projected world oil consumption in 2020 is about 120 million barrels a day—up 60 percent just from 1999.

THE ORIENT EXPRESS—CHINA, IRAN, AND THE UN SECURITY COUNCIL

The cover story of the June 20, 2005, *U.S. News and World Report* read: *The CHINA Challenge.* The key section of the magazine was devoted to articles related to the rise of China and what this may mean for the rest of the world economically, politically, culturally, and militarily. The third paragraph sets the serious tone of the article.

> The raw industry of the Chinese people has produced an economy growing faster than any other in modern history. China has become a juggernaut that is the world's second-largest purchaser of oil, and it will soon buy more cars, computers, and appliances than any other place on Earth. Perhaps more important: In its people and its policies, China today is infused with a profound sense of destiny, a steely determination to regain primacy in world affairs. The rest of the world is just beginning to digest what that might mean.[44]

China is being compared to the explosive growth in late nineteenth century America—except that it's happening on a faster and broader scale. China became a net oil importer in 1993. China is already the world's second largest consumer of oil, and its consumption increases by 7.5 percent a year, seven times faster than the U.S. This means China's thirst for oil will increase by 150 percent by 2020. By 2030 China's oil imports will equal those in the U.S. In this same year it's projected that China will surpass the U.S. in its number of cars. By 2010 China will have ninety times more cars than it had just in 1990.

At present, China imports about 10 percent of its oil from Iran. But that may be increasing dramatically very soon. *The Associated Press* has reported that the China Petrochemical Corporation has made a deal with Iran potentially worth $100 billion to develop Iran's massive Yadavaran oil field. Iran is making this move to cover its bases as it faces the prospect of sanctions over its nuclear program.[45]

There's a very important twist to all this—China has a veto on the UN Security Council. China has veto power over any UN actions against Iran at the same time they are dependent on Iranian crude oil and making huge oil deals with Iran. A greater conflict of interest could hardly be imagined.

China and Russia have consistently obstructed any sanctions or action against Iran that have any teeth to them. The reason, or at least part of it, is clear. China needs Iran's oil. If Iran cut China off, there simply isn't another market to take up the slack for China's increasing oil thirst. There's only so much oil to go around. What this means, according to Tertzakian, is that, "the United States is now more dependent and less secure than ever, just as China has recently emerged as America's competition in the great oil scramble of the new century."[46]

BARRELING TOWARD CRISIS

Most of the world's proven oil reserves lie under the sands of the turbulent Middle East. This means that the main oil resources of the world are concentrated in the most vulnerable region. This is not a good combination.

In this current climate, rogue, oil-producing nations like Iran can use oil to blackmail the world. Iran can pursue her nuclear ambitions with impunity as she confidently holds the ever-important oil card.

Iran continuously threatens the U.S. with "harm and pain" if we lead the world to put sanctions on Iran or if we initiate military attacks on her nuclear facilities. While part of this "harm and pain" could be terrorist attacks against foreign U.S. interests or even on U.S. soil, one has to believe that oil figures into Iran's plan. After all, just the escalation of the crisis in Iran has brought about an increase in the price of crude oil on the world market.

Any proposed economic sanctions or military action by the European Union or the United States must be carefully weighed against the effect this will have on world oil supply. Iran has a major influence on world oil markets. In April 2006 oil hit $75 a barrel for the first time, over fears about the Iran crisis.

Iran only pumps about 4 million barrels of crude a day or about 5 percent of the world's daily need. However, Iran is the second largest oil producer among the eleven members of OPEC, and the world's fourth largest exporter of crude oil. Also, Iran says that it plans to up its production from 4 to 7 million barrels a day in the next twenty years, giving it an even larger share of the world's exports and greater clout. Although the U.S. does not purchase Iranian oil, the narrow margin in the world between supply and demand would be profoundly affected, at least in the short term, by any Iranian embargo or cut in production, and the price of oil on the world market could rise substantially.

Iran could not only cut or limit its own production, it could also direct terror or military attacks against key oil sites in neighboring Saudi Arabia. Back in February 2006, several al Qaeda suicide bombers tried to take out the huge eastern Saudi Arabian site at Alqaiq. If the U.S. or a U.S.-led coalition executes a military strike against Iran, it could retaliate by hitting key Saudi oil sites. The economic consequence would be devastating for the West, since Saudi Arabia is the world's number one exporter of oil.

"STRAIT" TALK ABOUT OIL

The Strait of Hormuz is a narrow strait that's the only sea passage to the open ocean for the Persian Gulf nations. The strait is located between Iran and the United Arab Emirates. It's twenty-one miles wide at its narrowest point, but has only two one-mile wide channels for sea traffic. These two travel channels are separated by a two-mile buffer zone.

In 2004, about 17 million barrels of oil a day navigated their way through the Strait of Hormuz. Today the best estimates are about 15–16.5 million barrels a day. This represents about 20 percent of the world's daily oil supply. Supplies from Saudi Arabia, Kuwait, Iraq, and Iran must pass through this narrow strait. Remember that these four nations have almost two-thirds of the world's proven oil reserves. And the oil that travels through that narrow waterway represents almost all of the world's spare capacity.

This means that Iran is the daily gatekeeper for 20 percent of the world's daily oil supply. Iran overlooks the strategic world oil chokepoint on the Strait of Hormuz. This means that Iran could not only cut her own oil production as a means of retaliation, but she could also shut down the strait. Experts believe that Iran already has a strategic plan in place to execute suicide attacks on U.S. military vessels in the Persian Gulf. In April 2006, Iran's elite Revolutionary Guards conducted war games in the Strait of Hormuz. These maneuvers were code named the "Holy Prophet" war games. Iran claims that it tested the world's fastest torpedo, with a speed of 223 mph. The Iranian-made torpedo is called the "Hoot" or "whale" and is designed to destroy large warships and submarines.

Also, the narrow strait could easily be shut down simply by the placement of a few sea mines in the narrow lanes. Iran currently possesses EM-53 bottom-tethered mines that it purchased from China in the 1990s. The navy says that it could take months to locate and remove these mines. And just think what would happen if Iran sunk a couple of full oil supertankers in the strait. It would be disastrous. The environmental effects would be far-reaching, and oil prices would skyrocket overnight. With 20 percent of the world's oil supply cut off indefinitely, the world economy would plunge into the financial abyss.

OIL AND THE END TIMES

As you can see from all this, Iran and other Middle Eastern nations have the U.S. and Europe in a very bad spot. Western nations are painfully aware of this dilemma. At any time, Iran can tighten the noose around our neck. They can cut production, disrupt oil flow through the Strait of Hormuz, institute some kind of embargo, or even take out Saudi production. With this in mind, our leaders face a delicate balance. They must deal firmly with terrorist states like Iran and their pursuit of nuclear weapons, but on the flip side they must be careful not to unnecessarily jeopardize our oil-dependent economy.

Iran will surely use oil in one way or another as an economic weapon to cause "harm and pain" if they decide this is in their best interest in the current standoff. Oil is a key dynamic that makes the Middle East and the current Iran crisis the number one predicament in the world today. Nations like Iran know that the oil won't last forever. It's a non-renewable resource. Now is their window of opportunity. If they want to attain their goals, they know that they must act quickly.

This is another factor that prefigures the end-time state of affairs depicted in the Bible and suggests that the coming of Christ could be very near.

CHAPTER 9

HOW LONG WILL THE U.S. AND ISRAEL WAIT?

*This notion that the United States is getting ready to attack Iran
is ridiculous. Having said that, all options are on the table.*

PRESIDENT GEORGE W. BUSH

In his State of the Union address in January 2002, President Bush identified three nations as the axis of evil in our world today: Iraq, Iran, and North Korea. President Bush said, "States like these, and their terrorist allies, constitute an axis of evil, arming to threaten the peace of the world. By seeking weapons of mass destruction these regimes pose a grave and growing danger. They could provide these arms to terrorists, giving them the means to match their hatred." With her radical Islamic agenda, terror network, pursuit of atomic weapons, and warhead plans, Iran has quickly moved to the center of the axis.

Some have drawn comparisons between the current stand-off and the Cuban missile crisis of the early 1960s. The Cuban missile crisis was undoubtedly one of the tensest moments in U.S. history, but it pales in comparison to the Iran nuclear threat. The Russians were at least considered to be rational and were kept in check by the idea of mutually assured destruction. But a nuclear Iran could mean nuclear proliferation through-out the entire region and would certainly mean the transfer of nuclear devices to madmen whose vengeance would know no bounds.

This raises the unavoidable question—how will the United States respond? How long will we wait to launch a preemptive strike to cripple Iran's nuclear ambitions? How much longer can we wait?

WHAT WILL AMERICA DO?

According to a Gallup poll from February 6 to 9, 2006, Iran replaced Iraq as the nation that most Americans consider to be their greatest enemy. In the poll, 31 percent of Americans listed Iran as their worst enemy, up 14 percent just from last year. Iraq was second with 21 percent (the same total as last year). And North Korea was a distant third with 15 percent.[47]

In spite of persistent disillusionment with the war in Iraq, a majority of Americans support military intervention in Iran if that country continues to produce material that can be used to develop nuclear weapons. A Los Angeles Times/Bloomberg poll conducted in January 2006 found that 57 percent of Americans back a hit on Iran if Iran's Islamic government pursues a program that could enable it to build nuclear arms.

President Bush has repeatedly made it clear that the United States cannot allow Iran to possess nuclear weapons. In a speech on the war on terror, on February 25, 2006, Bush accused Iran of sponsoring terrorism and said, "A non-transparent society that is the world's premier state sponsor of terror cannot be allowed to possess the world's most dangerous weapons." The threat of a nuclear Iran has moved to the top of the international agenda for the White House.

The Pentagon has begun drawing up an extensive strategy

for dealing with Iran if, but more likely when, diplomatic negotiations fail.

Pentagon strategists are drawing up plans for bombing raids backed by submarine-launched ballistic missile attacks on Iran's nuclear sites as a 'last resort' to block Tehran's suspected efforts to develop an atomic bomb. United States Central Command and Strategic Command planners are identifying targets, assessing weapon loads and working on logistics for an operation. They are reporting to the office of the Defense Secretary, Donald Rumsfeld, as the U.S. updates plans for action if the diplomatic offensive fails to thwart Iran's nuclear ambitions. Tehran says it is developing only a civilian energy program. 'This is more than just the standard military contingency assessment,' a senior Pentagon adviser said. 'This has taken on much greater urgency in recent months.' The prospect of military action could put Washington at odds with Britain, which fears an attack would spark more violence in the Middle East and reprisals in the West and might not cripple Tehran's nuclear program. But the steady flow of disclosures about Iran's secret nuclear operations and the virulent anti-Israeli threats of its President, Mahmoud Ahmadinejad, has prompted the fresh assessment of military options by the US. The most likely strategy would involve aerial bombardment by long-distance B2 bombers, each armed with up to 18,000 kilograms of precision weapons, including the latest bunker-busting devices. They would fly from bases in Missouri and refuel in flight. The Bush

Administration has recently announced plans to add conventional ballistic missiles to the armoury of its nuclear Trident submarines within the next two years. If ready in time, they would also form part of the plan of attack.[48]

Many believe that the U.S. military already has a specific strategy in place to launch a preemptive strike and take out the Iranian nuclear sites. It's called "Global Strike." Here are the basics of this strategy:

Global strike, formally known as CONPLAN 8022, refers to a specific set of contingencies to attack weapons of mass destruction should diplomacy fail in a crisis or if there are intelligence warnings of preparations for any type of strike on the United States or one of its allies. Practically, the global strike war plan applies to Iran and North Korea. Global strike differs from other existing war plans—even for those two countries—in that it does not posit a U.S. response to invasion. That would be a defensive U.S. response. Instead, global strike constitutes a bolt-out-of-the-blue attack, a capability that has been developed wherein the President could order an attack within hours. Since at least the middle of 2004, U.S. long-range bombers and submarines have been on alert to carry out an attack on weapons of mass destruction targets that could potentially threaten the United States. At Strategic Command (STRATCOM) in Omaha, the global strike plan has been written and refined. The choreography for bomber and cruise missile attacks has been arranged. Actual targets have been selected, and WMD activity is monitored, resulting in constant revisions of the choreography.[49]

In March 2006, Sam Gardiner, a military strategy expert who has taught at the U.S. Army's National War College said, "I think we may be looking at a [U.S.] decision in six to nine months."

Here are a couple of excerpts from the president's 49-page National Security Strategy released in March 2006.

IRAN: "We may face no greater challenge from a single country than from Iran. For almost 20 years, the Iranian regime hid many of its key nuclear efforts from the international community, yet the regime continues to claim that it does not seek to develop nuclear weapons. The United States has joined with our European Union partners and Russia to pressure Iran to meet its international obligations and provide objective guarantees that its nuclear program is only for peaceful purposes. This diplomatic effort must succeed if confrontation is to be avoided."

STRIKE-FIRST POLICY: "There are few greater threats than a terrorist attack with weapons of mass destruction. To forestall or prevent such hostile acts by our adversaries, the United States will, if necessary, act pre-emptively in exercising our inherent right of self-defense. The United States will not resort to force in all cases to pre-empt emerging threats. Our preference is that nonmilitary actions succeed. And no country should ever use pre-emptions as a pretext for aggression."

If the U.S. hits Iran's nuclear facilities, there will certainly be serious consequences. Iran has promised "harm and pain" will result from any attack. At least three of these consequences immediately come to mind. First, Iran has threatened to unleash its terror network on U.S., international, and domestic targets. Second, Iran would probably also play the oil card as we saw in chapter 8. This would send the price of oil through the roof and would have a dire effect on the U.S. economy. Third, the U.S. would probably lose even more political and diplomatic ground in its relations with Middle Eastern nations. The consequences present real challenges for our government. But as Senator John McCain said recently: "There is only one thing worse than the U.S. exercising a military option (against Iran), and that is a nuclear-armed Iran."

No human being knows for sure what America will do or when she will do it. But if we take the president's comments seriously, we will act militarily to stop Iran from acquiring nuclear weapons if the diplomatic channels fail. And if we are to act, it must be soon.

When this happens, the stage-setting for the end times could experience a kind of prophetic shift of gears. But this may be nothing compared to what would happen if Israel hits Iran's nuclear facilities.

HOW LONG WILL ISRAEL WAIT?

This may be the key question in this present crisis. Israel has repeatedly made it crystal clear that she cannot and will not allow Iran to obtain nuclear weapons. Israel has a history of willingness to make a preemptive strike against nuclear plants.

On June 7, 1981, Israel shocked the world by taking out an Iraqi nuclear reactor. Prime Minister Menachem Begin ordered the strike on a French-built nuclear plant in Osirak, eighteen miles south of Baghdad. Israeli F-15 bombers and F-16 fighters destroyed the 70-megawatt uranium-powered reactor.

Israel has vowed that it will do the same thing to the Iranian reactors if the world doesn't act. When Israeli General Halutz was asked, "How far would Israel go to stop Iran's nuclear program?" he calmly responded, "2000 kilometers." That's the distance from Israel to Iran.

Israel already has plans for the attack on Iran. In November 2003, Israel's Defense Minister, Shaul Mofaz said that an Iranian nuclear weapon was "intolerable" and warned that "only a few months are left for Israel and the world to take action and prevent Iran from getting the nuclear bomb."[50]

On January 24, 2005, Meir Dagan, director of the Israeli Mossad, said that "by the end of 2005 the Iranians will reach the point of no return from the technological perspective of creating a uranium-enrichment capability." He added that once you have that capability, "you are home free."[51] Other sources in Israel have said publicly that they believe Iran reached "the point of no return" in their nuclear program at the end of March 2006.[52]

In March 2006, I heard an Israeli leader publicly state on Fox News that Israel would act within one year if Iran's nuclear capability is not dismantled or destroyed by someone else.

It's believed that if Israel exercises the military option, both air and ground forces will be utilized in an all-out effort to set

Iran's nuclear program back for years. Israel would probably call on Unit 262, its top special forces brigade, to execute the ground attack. Israeli special forces were placed on "G" readiness—the highest stage—beginning as early as December 2005.[53]

The Iranian assault would be much more difficult than the 1981 attack against the Iraqi nuclear plant. The Israeli planes would probably have to be granted permission by the U.S. to fly over Iraqi airspace. And there are presently seven nuclear plants in Iran, not one. Tehran seems to have learned a critical lesson from the Iraqi nuclear plant bombing: have multiple sites, not just one.

Nevertheless, Israeli military officials say that they can travel the 2000 kilometers to Iran and back without refueling and speak confidently of their odds for success. However, the only Israeli planes that can make the trip without refueling are its twenty-five F-151 strike fighters (69 Squadron) and because of the large amount of fuel they would have to carry, they couldn't carry as much ordnance. It might be impossible for Israel to destroy all of Iran's nuclear sites in one raid as they did in Iraq.[54]

But whatever the outcome, there's every indication that Israel may not be able to wait much longer.

SET-UP FOR THE FUTURE

If the U.S. hits Iran's nuclear targets, the cleavage between the U.S. and the nations of the Middle East will widen. This will continue to drive these nations to ally themselves even more closely with one another and probably Russia. Moreover, Iran has already threatened that if the U.S. attacks its nuclear sites, its first retaliatory strike will be against Israel.

If Israel strikes, the anti-Semitic backlash will be horrendous. Ahmadinejad already has a devilish hatred for Israel. Just think how he would go off if Israel stalled his nuclear program.

Any military action by the U.S. and/or Israel against Iran would undoubtedly plant seeds of vengeful animosity in Iran that could later erupt in the fulfillment of Ezekiel 38–39. We may be witnessing the stage-setting for this incredible prophecy right now!

PART THREE

IRAN'S FUTURE—THE FINAL JIHAD

From 1996 to 2000 there was a popular television program named *Early Edition*. The plot outline of the show was quite simple. The main character, named Gary Hobson, received the next day's newspaper a day early. He received tomorrow's newspaper today. He didn't know how. He didn't know why. All he knew was that from the time the early edition hit his doorstep, he had 24 hours to act to prevent terrible things from happening.

When you think about it, God's prophetic Word found in the Bible is our "early edition" of future events. It's like having tomorrow's newspaper today. While this early edition doesn't tell us everything or answer all our questions, it does provide us with the headlines of the future.

I think you'll be amazed at what this early edition says about the future of Iran and the Middle East, and how events in our world today bear an amazing correspondence to the prophecies of the Bible.

However, perhaps you'll be more amazed to discover what the Bible *doesn't* say and why. Why, for example, do the prophets seem strangely silent regarding the role of America in the end-times? Could it be that the U.S. taking military action against Iran to debilitate its nuclear capacity pushes Iran into executing a final, possibly even a nuclear, blow against the U.S.? Or could there be some other explanation for the prophet's silence?

Before we consider Iran's future as recorded in Ezekiel 38–39, let's pause and answer these pressing questions.

CHAPTER 10

WILL AMERICA SURVIVE?

There may now be a window of opportunity for
effective preventive action, but this window is more likely
to be measured in months than years.
MORTIMER B. ZUCKERMAN

The U.S. is waist deep in its war against terror,
and Iran is the world's worst state sponsor of terrorism.
Iran's nuclear program makes it much worse. Like a bad nightmare,
Iran's nuclear program plagues us night after night.
KENNETH POLLACK, *THE PERSIAN PUZZLE*

On September 12, 2001, Peggy Noonan, a *Wall Street Journal* columnist wrote that New Yorkers who were still alive should be thankful to be alive and thankful that "for some reason, and we don't even know what it was, the terrorists didn't use a small nuclear weapon floated into New York on a barge in the East River." She said, "We are lucky that this didn't turn nuclear, chemical or biological. It could have, and I thought the next time the bad guys hit it would have. Instead they used more 'conventional' weapons, fuel-heavy airliners and suicide bombers. And so the number of dead will be in the thousands or tens of thousands and not millions or tens of millions." Noonan warned that "for now we have been spared. And now, chastened and shaken, we are given another chance,

119

maybe the last chance, to commit ourselves seriously and at some cost to protecting our country."[55]

Since the terrorist attacks of 9/11, our world has changed dramatically. We live in an age of color-coded terror alerts, painstaking airport security, and rigorous security checks at sporting events.

In this new era, we have all wondered if the nuclear threat could reach our soil. We wondered if Iraq and Saddam Hussein could pose such a threat—if Iraq could pass a nuclear device to some terror cell to strike on American soil. With that threat defused, we now face the nuclear threat posed by Iran and its terror network. The threat has now become more real than ever.

This kind of sobering, yet realistic thinking causes many people to wonder what will happen to America. Will we be a major player in the end times? Will we be taken out by a nuclear attack? Does the Bible tell us anything about America's role in final drama?

Almost everyone is interested in how the United States fits into end-time prophecies.

NO MENTION OF AMERICA IN BIBLE PROPHECY

Everyone agrees that America is not mentioned specifically by name in the Bible. However, over the years, some prophecy teachers have found places in the Bible that they believe describe the United States. Some believe that America is the unnamed nation in Isaiah 18. Others believe that "the young lions of Tarshish" in Ezekiel 38:13 is a veiled reference to America. Still others maintain that America, or New York City, is Babylon the Great, the great prostitute city, in Revelation

17–18. Having carefully studied each of these passages in its context, I don't believe that any of them refer to America. I believe that the Bible is silent about America's role in the end times.

But this raises another question—why isn't America mentioned as a key player in the events of the end times? We are undoubtedly the greatest nation in human history in terms of political, economic, and military might. It seems strange that the U.S. would not merit at least some passing mention in the biblical passages where end-time events are described. Of course, most modern nations aren't mentioned in the Bible; therefore, it could just be that God has chosen not to mention America. However, if we are still the world's number-one power when the end times arrive, it does seem strange for us to be totally absent. So, how do we explain this deafening biblical silence about America's role in the final years of this age?

THE LATE GREAT UNITED STATES?

Many now believe that the reason America is absent from Bible prophecy is that we will be taken out by nuclear terror. As things now stand, this is certainly a distinct possibility. The detonation of a nuclear device in any of America's crowded urban areas, especially New York City would totally devastate our nation. The economy would immediately collapse. We would be left numb and irreversibly damaged.

If Iran is allowed to obtain nuclear weapons and were to pass a suitcase-sized nuclear bomb to a terrorist cell, this nightmare could become a reality, and one could easily imagine that America would retreat from the rest of the world, adopting a policy of isolation. Or even pass into oblivion.

BUSH AND KERRY AGREE

In the first presidential debate for the 2004 election, George Bush and John Kerry didn't agree on very much. However, when asked to define the "single most serious threat to American national security," both unhesitatingly answered, "nuclear terrorism." President Bush said, "I agree with my opponent that the biggest threat facing the country is weapons of mass destruction in the hands of a terrorist network."

Since 2004, the other key figures in the Bush administration have all echoed this sentiment. The greatest threat to America today is not nuclear missiles flying through the sky, but nuclear packages smuggled into the United States by terrorists on a container ship or carried with drugs across the porous Mexican border. And Iran poses the gravest threat for this danger.

LIVING ON BORROWED TIME?

Is the nuclear threat against America really that great? If you believe al Qaeda it is. Only nine months after the attack on New York City on 9/11, Sulaiman Abu Gheith, Osama bin Laden's official press spokesmen, boldly announced "We have the right to kill 4 million Americans, including 1 million children."[56] Four million. The only way to kill four million Americans is by detonating a nuclear weapon in an urban area. This alleged right to murder four million Americans, according to Abu Gheith, comes from the casualties allegedly inflicted on Muslims by America and Israel. In light of the ongoing war in Iraq, Islamic terrorists must believe they now have the right to kill even more Americans, and Iran is the only radical Muslim nation with the potential to produce a nuclear bomb that would kill millions.

Director of U.S. Intelligence Porter Goss has communicated to the Senate Intelligence Committee that there is enough nuclear material missing from Russia to make a bomb, and that he has no idea where it is. If this material makes its way to Iran, the result will be disastrous. It would greatly accelerate Iran's timetable for constructing a nuclear weapon.

Harvard professor Graham Allison has written a book titled *Nuclear Terrorism*. He believes that on the current path, a nuclear attack on U.S. soil within the next ten years is "more likely than not."[57] Former Secretary of Defense William Perry lays the odds for a nuclear attack on American soil at 50–50 by 2010.[58]

If nuclear terror does hit America, the scenarios are utterly apocalyptic. Marvin Olasky, editor in chief of *World* magazine, provides this graphic description:

> We can start by realizing that a 10-kiloton bomb exploded at the Smithsonian (the Hiroshima bomb was a 12-kiloton) would destroy everything from the White House to the Capitol building, with uncontrollable fires raging all the way to the Pentagon. In other cities as well every body and building up to one-third of a mile from the epicenter would vanish, and everything up to one and one-half miles away would be destroyed by fires and radiation. A report in 2003 by the Energy Department's National Nuclear Security Administration estimated that a Washington, D.C., nuclear explosion could kill 300,000 persons. A report in 2004 by the Homeland Security Council (HSC) used different assumptions and came up with a number of 'only' 100,000. The HSC report noted that it

would take years to clean up 3,000 to 5,000 square miles around a nuclear explosion, with many irradiated neighborhoods simply abandoned: A nuclear attack 'would forever change the American psyche, its politics and worldview.'[59]

In a poll taken in 2003, four out every ten Americans say that they "often worry about the chances of a nuclear attack by terrorists."[60] I bet it's much higher than that by now.

THE DIRTY BOMB OPTION

Even if terrorists can be kept from gaining access to nuclear weapons, they have a deadly fallback position: a dirty bomb. A so-called dirty bomb is an ordinary explosive device wrapped together with a chunk of radioactive material. A dirty bomb could be something as simple as a stick of dynamite in a shoe box of radioactive material.

According to Graham Allison, a dirty bomb is a "weapon of mass disruption," not a weapon of mass destruction because it would not immediately cause mass devastation and death.

The main negative results of a dirty bomb would be mass panic and the cost of decontamination.[61]

Detonating such a device in a densely populated area could potentially kill thousands, but its main havoc would be the long-term effect of making an area of several square miles uninhabitable for months or longer. Marvin Olasky vividly describes the grim aftermath of a dirty-bomb explosion.

An explosion in a crowded area could kill several thousand and make at least several square miles of prime real estate unusable. A cobalt radiation bomb exploded in Manhattan could require the evacuation of the entire island, with people unable to come back safely for months.

The economic consequences of even a dirty bomb would be large, and the psychological consequences enormous. The anthrax scare late in 2001, like the Katrina disaster in 2005, led to panic and outrage about problems small in relation to those that would result from any kind of nuclear explosion.

Even if the U.S. is able to thwart the nuclear threat for the next few years, Iran could still pass nuclear material to a third party who could easily make a dirty bomb and set it off in the center of an American city. While we hope this never happens, many believe that such an attack is already overdue. As *World* magazine reports:

Terrorists undoubtedly relish the thoughts of wreaking such havoc, so it's remarkable that we haven't already had some kind of nuclear disaster. Interviewers for two years have asked Harvard's Allison why we have not had one, and his regular answers have been: 'It's a great puzzle.... I think that we should be very thankful that it hasn't happened already.... We're living on borrowed time.'

A string of dirty-bomb hits in major U.S. cities could so damage our national psyche and our economy that we would be driven inward and retreat from our place of world prominence.

AMERICA IN THE END TIMES

No one knows for sure what will happen to America in the future since the Bible is silent on the issue. As prophecy expert John Walvoord admits, "Any final answer to the question is therefore an impossibility, but nevertheless some conclusions of a general character can be reached."[62]

With this in mind, let me share with you the three main points of reasoning that lead me to "some conclusions of a general character."

FRIENDS OF ISRAEL

First, as things stand right now, I believe that America will remain strong until the time of the Rapture for one simple reason—Israel. We are Israel's chief ally and protector. Our economic and military aid to Israel each year totals somewhere in the neighborhood of $3–4 billion depending on which statistics you use. According to the Congressional Research Service, from 1949 to 2000 the United States has given Israel at total of $81.38 billion in aid. Others place the total as high as $91 billion. Depending on the numbers you use, about 20 percent of American foreign aid goes to Israel. American aid makes up 7–8 percent of the total Israeli national budget. The situation is clear—unless things change dramatically, without the United States, Israel would be incinerated in a matter of days by her hostile Arab neighbors. Since Israel is pictured in Scripture as a thriving, prosperous nation in the end times in Ezekiel 38, unless things change dramatically, I believe America must remain strong until the time of the Rapture to serve as Israel's chief ally.

ANTICHRIST STEPS IN

Second, we know from Scripture that after the Rapture, the Antichrist will come to Israel's side and make a seven-year treaty with her (Daniel 9:27). But where is America in that scenario? Why aren't we around as Israel's great protector?

Evidently, the Antichrist and his European empire will replace America as Israel's chief ally and as the major world power (see Daniel 2:44–45; 7:23–25). We'll talk more about this in the next chapter. This strong presence of Europe indicates to me that something will have happened to America that shifts world power back to Europe.

THE RAPTURE FACTOR

Third, if America must remain strong up to the time of the Rapture, but then after the Rapture is replaced by Europe as the world's superpower, then what does this tell us?

I believe it tells us that America will be brought to her knees by the Rapture. The Rapture is the key. The Rapture changes everything.

Think about it: If the Rapture were to happen today, if all the true believers in Jesus Christ were whisked away to heaven in a split second, America would be devastated beyond comprehension. Consider these most recent statistics from Barna Research Online:

Eighty-five percent of Americans claim to be Christians. This group is often identified as "cultural Christians."

Forty-one percent of Americans claim to be "born-again Christians."

Seven percent of American adults are identified as "evangelical Christians." This group is a subset of the "born-again" group. The main factor in this category is a belief that salvation is by faith in Christ alone without human works. According to Barna, this represents about 14–16 million American adults. Adding in children, the number could easily climb to 25–30 million.

The total population of America according to the 2000 census is 281,421,906. At least 25 million are believers in Christ or are small children of believers. That's how many Americans will disappear all at once when the Rapture occurs. The impact will be nothing short of cataclysmic. Not only would our country lose about 10 percent of her population, but she would lose the "salt and light" of this great land (Matthew 5:13–14).

The immediate ripple effect will touch every area of our society. Millions of mortgages will go unpaid, military personnel by the thousands will be permanently AWOL, factory workers will never show up for work again, college tuition will go unpaid, businesses will be left without workers and leaders, the Dow will crash, the NASDAQ will plummet, and the entire economy will be thrown into chaos.

Charles Dyer, author of several excellent books on end-time prophecy, describes the impact of the Rapture on America.

Today as many as half of all Americans claim to be 'born again,' or believers in Jesus Christ. If only one-fourth of that number have genuinely made a personal commitment to Christ, then over 28 million Americans will suddenly 'disappear' when God removes his church from the earth. Can you imagine the effects on our country if over 28 million people—

people in industry, government, the military, business, agriculture, education, medicine and communications—disappear? That is approximately double the entire population of New York City, Los Angeles, Chicago, and Houston all rolled together! The economic fluctuations of the eighties and even the Great Depression will pale in comparison to the political and economic collapse that will occur when our society suddenly loses individuals who were its 'salt and light.' America could not support an army in the Middle East because the military would be needed at home to control the chaos![63]

The Rapture may well be the end of America as we know it. Those who miss out on the Rapture in the United States will be left behind to pick up the pieces.

SOME FINAL CONCLUSIONS

Does this mean that America will be spared a nuclear attack? Only God knows the answer to that question. Certainly it is possible that America will suffer some catastrophic devastation at the hands of terrorists. Possibly a dirty bomb. Or even a nuclear attack. There may be many twists and turns between now and the beginning of the end times that no person could foresee. But as things stand right now, here are seven general conclusions I've reached about America's future role.

1. America is not mentioned in the Bible.
2. America is Israel's main defender.
3. America must remain strong until the end times to continue her defense of Israel.

4. The Scriptural silence concerning America in the end times indicates that America will fall from her position of world prominence.
5. World power in the end times is centered in the Reunited Roman Empire (Europe). (More about this in the next chapter.)
6. European prominence can only be explained in light of U.S. decline.
7. The U.S. will suffer her decline, her fall, at the Rapture of the church.

The current Iran crisis will test U.S. resolve unlike any situation the nation has ever faced. How and when the U.S. responds may determine its future. But in our troubled, uncertain world, we can rest in the knowledge that the ultimate destiny of America and every nation is in God's hands.

CHAPTER 11

EUROPE'S BID FOR WORLD PEACE

Europeans want to preserve and nurture their cultural heritage,
enjoy a good quality of life in the here and now,
and create a sustainable world of peace in the near or
not too distant future.

JEREMY RIFKIN, *THE EUROPEAN DREAM*

When I was growing up in the '60s and '70s there were two great military powers in the world: the United States and the Soviet Union. While the Soviet Union was a great menace, the presence of these two superpowers created a certain balance of power in the world.

We used to think that if the Soviet Union collapsed the world would be a much safer place. Were we ever wrong! Since the dissolution of the Soviet Union in 1991, the world has become an increasingly more dangerous place. Sadly, a look at the world scene today makes the cold war era look like the "good ol' days."

There are no longer two key players in the balance of power formula—there seem to be dozens. The world is more at risk today for nuclear detonations, and biological and chemical warfare than ever before. Nine nations have the bomb, and it is only a matter of time until rogue states, terrorists, or fanatics get their hands on these weapons of mass destruction. The Iran nuclear crisis along with the escalating foment in key Islamic nations could easily erupt into an explosive call for widespread jihad or holy war inciting terror attacks and the resulting oil shortages.

The great need in our uncertain world today is peace and safety. People the world over are clamoring for peace—peace in the Balkans, peace in strife-torn African nations, but most of all, peace in the Middle East. We want a peaceful world in which to prosper and raise our families.

People are also yearning for safety. We have never felt more unsafe, more exposed, more vulnerable, than we do right now. We want safety. Safety for ourselves. Safety for our children. Safety from a nuclear nightmare, safety from terrorist bombings, safety from bioterrorism, safety from chemical warfare.

Of course, this longing is nothing new. But with the rise of war by stealth—the sudden, unexpected strike of terrorism— the cry for peace and safety has become a worldwide cadence. The only solution is some sort of peace treaty that ends the threat of terrorism, solves the Iran nuclear crisis, brings peace between Israel and the Palestinians, and secures the uninterrupted flow of oil to the West whose survival depends on a steady supply of oil.

Amazingly, the Bible predicts that someday the world will finally achieve peace *and* safety. In 1 Thessalonians 5:3, the Scripture says that a day is coming when people everywhere will be saying, "Peace and safety!"

How will this ever be achieved? Frankly, right now it looks impossible. Iran's president seems bent on getting his hands on nuclear weapons, destroying Israel, and creating worldwide chaos. But if peace were to come about from today's alignment of nations, who would we expect to be at the forefront of the negotiations? Europe. In all the peace negotiations in the world today,

Europe is taking the lead. With U.S. popularity and stature at an all-time low, Europe has filled the gap. Europe is quickly rising to the position of world peacemaker. The new European dream is to spread a utopian peace throughout the world.

Europe is deeply involved in the Israeli-Palestinian dilemma. The EU3—Britain, France, and Germany—led the negotiations and talks with Iran over its nuclear program. Even the U.S., in light of the war in Iraq, seems to have reluctantly accepted that it cannot act militarily without at least some measure of European approval. Europe is the world's undisputed leader in the peacemaking business.

And that's exactly the end-time role the Bible predicts for Europe and its final leader. The Bible says a man is coming who will broker the greatest peace deal in history. A man is coming who will give the world what it clamors for. He will even be able to placate unreasonable rulers like Mahmoud Ahmadinejad. This coming world ruler will rise from a final, reunited form of the Roman Empire or what we might call a European superstate.

The Bible calls this man the Antichrist. And the way appears to be paved for his rise.

MAN OF PEACE, MAN OF POWER

Most people don't realize that there are over one hundred passages in the Bible that detail the origin, nationality, career, character, kingdom, and final doom of the Antichrist.

I don't know what you think of when you hear the word *Antichrist.* Maybe you see him as a crazed madman, a diabolical fiend, a modern Adolph Hitler, or a shameless egomaniac. While all of these images are accurate, none of them picture what the Antichrist will be like when the world gets its first impression of him.

The Antichrist will come on the world-scene insignificantly at the beginning of his career. The initial, clear mention of him in the Bible is in Daniel 7:8 where he is called "a little horn." He will appear inconspicuously at first.

The first clue in Scripture as to the identity of the Antichrist is found in Daniel 9:27 where he is pictured as rising from a final form of the Roman Empire and brokering a treaty with Israel. "And he [Antichrist] will make a firm covenant with the many for one week [7 years]." This means that when the world gets its first glimpse of the Antichrist it will be as a great peacemaker. He will make a covenant with "the many" which in the context of Daniel 9:24 refers to a majority within the nation of Israel.

What is the exact nature of this covenant that the Antichrist will make with Israel? Charles Dyer, a respected prophecy teacher and author, says:

> What is this 'covenant' that the Antichrist will make with Israel? Daniel does not specify its content, but he does indicate that it will extend for seven years. During the first half of this time Israel feels at peace and secure, so the covenant must provide some guarantee for Israel's national security. Very likely the covenant will allow Israel to be at peace with her Arab neighbors. One result of the covenant is that Israel will be allowed to rebuild her temple in Jerusalem. This world ruler will succeed where Kissinger, Carter, Reagan, Bush, and other world leaders have failed. He will be known as the man of peace![64]

The Antichrist will come with the olive branch of peace in his hand. He will come on the scene and accomplish what was considered impossible. He will solve the Middle Eastern peace puzzle. He will rid the world of terrorism. He will be hailed as the greatest peacemaker who has ever lived.

You can just see it now. He will be *Time* Magazine's Person of the Year. He will win the Nobel Peace Prize.

RIDER ON THE WHITE HORSE

A further picture of the Antichrist's initial peaceful agenda is given in Revelation 6:2; the Antichrist is pictured as a rider on a white horse, a pseudo-Christ, who will ride on the world scene initially in the power of peace. "I looked, and behold, a white horse, and he who sat on it had a bow; and a crown was given to him, and he went out conquering and to conquer." Notice that he wears a victor's crown and has a bow, but no arrows. This symbolism seems to indicate that he will win a bloodless victory at the beginning of his career. The sword indicates the threat of war, but it never materializes because he is able to gain victory through peaceful negotiations. He will be the consummate negotiator and persuader. The peace that he brings to Israel will quickly spill over to the entire world. Amazingly, even nations like Iran and her fanatical allies will stand down in the face of this master diplomat.

He brings what the world wants more than anything else—worldwide peace and safety. We know that he ushers in a time of worldwide peace because the rider on the second horse in Revelation 6:3–4, the red horse, comes and takes peace from the earth. For peace to be taken from the earth it must exist.

THE EU—A REUNITED ROMAN EMPIRE

The Bible predicts in Daniel 2 and 7 that this final world ruler will arise from a Mediterranean coalition of nations out of the old Roman Empire. This final-world kingdom will be what many have called a revived or reunited Roman Empire. The final form of this end time empire will initially be ruled over by ten kings or leaders according to Daniel's prophecy. These ten leaders are pictured as the ten toes on the image in Daniel 2 and the ten horns on the final beast in Daniel 7.

Incredibly, over the last sixty years the nations of Europe have begun to come back together just as the Bible predicted.

There were three main triggers for the formation of the European Union. First, the United States emerged as the world's leading industrial nation. Europe eventually realized that it had to form some kind of union to keep up economically. Second, World Wars I and II convinced the nations of Europe that enough was enough. After centuries of battles and bloodshed that bathed the continent in blood, a new age was born. Cooperation replaced conflict. As best-selling author Jeremy Rifkin observes,

> The EU is novel in being the very first mega-governing institution in all of history to be born out of the ashes of defeat. Rather than commemorate a noble past, it sought to ensure that the past would never be repeated. After a thousand years of unremitting conflict, war, and bloodshed, the nations of Europe emerged from the shadows of the two world wars, in the span of less than half a century, decimated: their population maimed and killed, their ancient monuments and

infrastructure lying in ruins, their worldly treasures depleted, and their way of life destroyed. Determined that they would never again take up arms against one another, the nations of Europe searched for a political mechanism that could bring them together and move them beyond their ancient rivalries.[65]

Third, the great colonial empires of European nations all ended in less than a single lifetime from about 1930 to 1997 (when Britain handed Hong Kong back to China).[66] In his *New York Times* bestseller, *The United States of Europe*, T. R. Reid describes how this motivated the nations of Europe to join together. "The loss of empire, then, brought with it not only the loss of a key trading market but also the demise of a certain stature, a certain sense of importance on the world stage, that had marked Europe's long colonial era. Looking for a new source of trading income and a new platform from which to reclaim their former global eminence, the former colonial powers found both gold and glory in their new European Union."[67]

The new age of peace and cooperation for Europe was officially inaugurated in March 1957 by the formation of the Common Market or European Economic Community. In a ceremony in Rome, six nations signed the Treaty of Rome. It's fitting that the document that began the entire process of the reuniting of the Roman Empire was called the "Treaty of Rome."

Since 1957, nation after nation has come together, until in 1992 the Maastricht Treaty signaled the birth of the European Union. This chart is a brief sketch of some of the key events and dates of the reuniting of the Roman Empire.

AN OVERVIEW OF THE REUNITING OF EUROPE

Establishment of the European Coal and Steel Community (ECSC) by signing the Treaty of Paris by six European nations.	1951
Birth of the modern EU (Treaty of Rome). Six nations: Belgium, Germany, Luxembourg, France, Italy, and the Netherlands (Total of 220 million people).	1957
EEC (European Economic Community) formed: Denmark, Ireland, and Great Britain join, bringing 66 million more people.	1973
Greece joins the EEC, becoming the tenth member.	1981
Portugal and Spain join the EEC.	1986
Signing of the Single European Act (SEA).	1986
Official formation of the EU	February 7, 1992
Austria, Finland, and Sweden join the EU, bringing the total population to 362 million in 15 members.	1995
Treaty of Amsterdam.	1997

Formation of the Monetary Union of the EU with currency called the euro. Eleven nations adopted the euro on January 1, 1999. Greece followed suit on January 1, 2001.	1999-2001
Treaty of Nice.	2000
Euro currency officially issued. This becomes known as E-day.	January 1, 2002
In the shadow of the ancient acropolis in Athens, Greece, ten more nations signed treaties to join the EU: Cyprus, the Czech Republic, Estonia, Hungary, Latvia, Lithuania, Malta, Poland, Slovakia, and Slovenia. The population of the EU was raised to almost half a billion.	April 16, 2004
Twenty-five-member nations signed the new EU constitution, amid great pomp, at a ceremony on Capitoline Hill in Rome.	October 29, 2004
The EU3 (Britain, France, and Germany) carried on extensive negotiations with Iran over its nuclear program.	2004-2006

In his bestselling book, Reid graphically chronicles the rise
and influence of the modern European superstate. He opens
his book with these words: "At the dawn of the twenty-first
century, a geopolitical revolution of historic dimensions is
under way across the Atlantic: the unification of Europe.
Twenty-five nations have joined together—with another dozen
or so on the waiting list—to build a common economy, government, and culture. Europe is a more integrated place today
than at any time since the Roman empire."[68]

Jeremy Rifkin says the same thing. "The only faint historical parallel to the EU is the Holy Roman Empire of the eighth
to early nineteenth centuries." Did you catch that? The new
integrated Europe is being compared by modern experts to the
Roman Empire. The European superstate appears to be a
reuniting of the Roman Empire in progress.

Consider these facts about the EU.

- It has more people (almost half a billion), more
  wealth, and more trade than the U.S. The EU has 7
  percent of the world's total population.

- It is the largest internal single market and largest trader
  of goods in the world.

- It has more votes in every international organization
  than the U.S.

- It gives away more money in development aid, resulting in global economic and political clout.

- It stretches from Ireland to Estonia.

- It has a president, parliament, cabinet, central bank, bill of rights, unified patent office, court system, and 80,000 page legal code.

- It has a 60,000-member army that is independent of NATO.

- It has its own space agency with 200 satellites in orbit and a project to put a man on Mars before America can.

- It has a 220,000-person governmental bureaucracy.

- It has the world's strongest currency (the Euro).

- It had a Gross Domestic Product of $10.5 trillion in 2003, exceeding the GDP of the U.S. (Europe's GDP is 6.5 times larger than China's.)

- It has a standard license plate, birth certificate, and passport, a common lottery, its own flag, anthem, and motto ("Unity in diversity").

- It hopes to have a seat on the U.N. Security Council—replacing the United Kingdom and France.

- It has a 265-page Constitution without any reference to God, and only one single reference to private property.

- It plans to have a single foreign minister who will carry out foreign and defense policies.[69]

The European superstate has arrived. The current form of the EU doesn't match the biblical prophecy of the final form of the Roman Empire because it doesn't exist in a ten-leader form. However, what we see developing there today points toward the final fulfillment of Daniel's prophecy.

The modern European superstate is totally secular. Europe's rich Christian history has been deliberately erased. God has been intentionally omitted from any of the founding documents, further paving the way for the Antichrist's coming.

All that remains now is for this conglomerate to be arranged under the leadership of ten leaders or a ten-member ruling committee. We might call this group the original "Big Ten." The final world ruler, or Antichrist, will arise from within this godless, reunited Roman empire, will uproot three of these leaders, and then the remaining rulers will surrender their power to him (Daniel 7:8).

Under the proposed EU Constitution, the current presidency, that rotates every six months among the member nations, will be replaced by a president who will serve up to five years and will be responsible for establishing the EU's agenda.[70] This is a perfect setting for one man to eventually come to power and rule the final form of the reunited Roman Empire as the Bible predicts.

A NEW PAX ROMANA

As Europe grows in influence and power, she is basking in a kind of new *Pax Romana*, or what one might call a *Pax Europa*. After centuries of perpetual warfare, Europe has achieved peace. And Europe's great vision is to export this peace to the entire world. To bring what it has found to all the world. To create a world of harmony and peace. European foreign policy today is founded on this indispensable notion of spreading peace.

Europe's new constitution uses language of universalism throughout its text and makes it clear that the focus is the entire planet. The European Dream is a utopian concept of a Europe without borders

Jeremy Rifkin closes his book, *The European Dream*, with these words. "These are tumultuous times. Much of the world is going dark, leaving many human beings without clear direction. The European Dream is a beacon of light in a troubled world. It beckons us to a new age of inclusivity, diversity, quality of life, deep play, sustainability, universal human rights, the rights of nature, and *peace on Earth*. We used to say that the American dream is worthy dying for. The new European Dream is worth living for."[71]

This strikingly foreshadows the biblical prophecies of the role of the reunited Roman empire in the end times.

SATANIC SUPERMAN

You might be asking—how will the final world ruler be able to pull this off? How will he do what so many others have miserably failed to do? How will he be able to solve the Middle East crisis and eventually bring peace to the world? How will he be able to get irrational leaders like Mahmoud Ahmadinejad to submit to his overtures?

The Bible says that he will be totally energized and empowered by Satan himself. He will have the full power of the evil one behind him like no man who has ever lived. Revelation 13:2 says, "And the dragon [Satan] gave him [Antichrist] his power and his throne and great authority."

The Antichrist will possess all the qualities of all the great leaders who have ever lived, rolled into one man. To help us better envision what the Antichrist will be like, H. L. Willmington has provided this helpful analogy with American presidents. The coming world ruler will possess:

The leadership of a Washington and Lincoln

The eloquence of a Franklin Roosevelt

The charm of a Teddy Roosevelt

The charisma of a Kennedy

The popularity of an Ike

The political savvy of a Johnson

The intellect of a Jefferson[72]

Since he will be uniquely empowered by Satan, like his master, he will masquerade as an angel of light at first not revealing his true goal, which is world conquest. But at the mid-point of the seven-year tribulation, the mask of peace will come off, and the world will be plunged into the terrible darkness of the great tribulation.

SUDDEN DESTRUCTION

God will interrupt man's pseudo-peace with the outpouring of His wrath and the outbreak of war. As 1 Thessalonians 5:3

goes on to say, "When they are saying, 'Peace and safety!' then destruction will come upon them suddenly like labor pains upon a woman with child, and they will not escape."

Man's utopia won't last long. God will bring it to an abrupt end with the opening of the second seal judgment in Revelation 6:3–4. When the rider on the red horse gallops forth during the tribulation with a mighty sword in his hand, the world will be plunged into war and slaughter.

The Russian-Iranian invasion of Israel, that we will discuss in the next chapter, will be one of the great military campaigns that shatters this fragile peace. So much for man's ability to bring peace to the world in his own efforts.

THE EVENING NEWS

I don't believe that the ongoing hostilities between Israel and her neighbors, the Iran crisis, and the unending Middle East peace process are accidents. These events are setting the stage for the final peace process ushered in by the European super-state and its leader. As you read the paper each day and listen to the television news reports about the Middle East, remember that the Bible, in about 530 BC in Daniel 9:27, predicted that the final world ruler would come to power on a platform of peace. What could be more relevant in our world today!

Current events in the Middle East today point clearly toward the precise scenario outlined in the Bible. It's really amazing when you think about it. We have the privilege of witnessing the developing and unfolding of this sign of the times every day on TV. Events we see today seem to harmonize with what the Bible predicts for the climax of the ages.

IS ANTICHRIST WAITING IN THE WINGS?

The same world that rejected the true Christ and hung Him on a cross is ripe for the rise of the Antichrist. The world that rejected the Light of the World will gladly embrace the Prince of Darkness. The world that crucified the Prince of Peace will hail the Beast out of the Sea. The world that couldn't tolerate the presence of the Holy One will welcome the Man of Sin.

Why? Because man wants to run this world himself. Man wants to do things his own way—without God.

The world grows more dangerous as each day passes. Iran's President, who is on a frantic mission to acquire the bomb, regularly spews out threats against Israel and the U.S. The world terror network is a dangerous web with unseen, faceless enemies. The world clamors for someone who can bring peace and safety. We want peace. We want safety. We want the Middle East peace process to materialize. We want an end to terrorism. We want an uninterrupted supply of oil. We want a peaceful solution to the Iran crisis. And the world is committed to make it happen.

We are enamored with diplomatic negotiations, with coalitions and alliances. World leaders love to posture, plan, ponder, and propose. But usually with meager, momentary results. However, a man is coming who will be able to get things done. He will be a man of action. A man of accomplishments.

The world will welcome him with open arms.

The world will ultimately fall down at his feet and worship him as god.

And we can be sure that Satan will have his counterfeit Christ ready to spring into action when the time is right. Since Satan's goal is to rule over and be worshiped by the world, I believe that in every generation he has a man ready to bring onto the world scene and take control. In every generation he has *an* Antichrist ready to take over when the time is right. So we can be sure that he has a man somewhere on the scene right now, waiting in the wings to give the world what it wants.

Who knows? *The* Antichrist may be waiting in the wings right now. And in the seemingly impossible crises we face, the Antichrist, not the U.S., will solve the world's problems.

CHAPTER 12

RADICAL ISLAM'S WAR WITH THE WEST

Spurred by modernization, global politics is being reconfigured along cultural lines. Peoples and countries with similar cultures are coming together. Peoples and countries with different cultures are coming apart. Alignments defined by ideology and superpower relations are giving way to alignments defined by culture and civilization. Political boundaries increasingly are redrawn to coincide with cultural ones: ethnic, religious, and civilizational. Cultural communities are replacing Cold War blocs, and the fault lines between civilizations are becoming the central lines of conflict in global politics.

SAMUEL HUNTINGTON,
THE CLASH OF CIVILIZATIONS

According to the Bible, in the end times, the nations of the world will be broadly aligned into three basic coalitions. First, there will be what we might call the Western federation of nations, including primarily Europe and her Western allies. Second, as we will see in the next chapter, there will be a Northern-Southern coalition consisting of Russia and the Islamic nations of North Africa and the Middle East. Third, China and other Asian nations will make up what the Bible calls the "kings of the east" or an Eastern union of nations (Revelation 16:12).

This is precisely the situation that Samuel Huntington, in his book, *The Clash of Civilizations*, envisions in the future. He says, "The dangerous clashes of the future are likely to arise from the interaction of Western arrogance, Islamic intolerance, and Sinic assertiveness."[73] Huntington's three-fold division of civilizations is the West, the Middle East, and the Far East.

We will leave the issue of the Far East and its place in Bible prophecy for another time, but for now it's clear from many current events that the chasm is widening between East and West. Between Islam and the Western powers. And this is exactly what one would expect if the end times were near.

While there are many recent events that reveal the growing divide between the nations of the Middle East and the West, let's consider just a couple of developments that highlight the clash of civilizations.

FRANCE IS BURNING

For eleven nights running in the fall of 2005, France endured riots that eventually spread to 300 French cities. The trouble began on October 27, 2005, when three Muslim youths were chased by French police. The three attempted to elude police by seeking sanctuary in a power substation, and two of the young men were subsequently electrocuted. The other man was injured but survived. Muslims blamed the police for their deaths, claiming that they purposely cornered the men in the substation. This event immediately sparked riots in the low-income Paris suburb of Clichy-sous-Bois. The rioters were primarily youths born of Arab and African immigrants in poor suburbs. These areas that are on the margins of society are fertile soil for Muslim extremists.

The main targets in the rioting were vehicles. In all, 4700

cars were torched. About 1400 vehicles were torched on one Sunday night alone (November 6, 2005). However, arsonists also burned two schools. Approximately 1,200 suspects were detained. The rioting eventually spilled over into Belgium and Germany.

France is home to five million Muslims, the largest population of Muslims in Western Europe. And while jihad may not be the inspiration for the rioters, it is undeniably an inseparable component, creating solidarity among the rioters. It appears that a full-fledged *intifada* ("uprising") unfolded on Paris's doorstep. In this entire episode there was a prevalent "us" versus "them" mentality on the part of the Muslim rioters. During the uprising one reporter stated that thousands of Muslims were shouting "Allahu Akbar" from windows of highrise apartment buildings. This exacerbated fears among some French citizens of an all-out Muslim revolution.

The flames of France served to further unveil the religio-cultural divide between East and West, and the lengths that Muslims would go to in order force the West to bow to their demands. French President Jacques Chirac passively admitted that the French were at fault for failing to fully integrate these immigrants into the larger society. Passive concessions were fine to temporarily quell the violence, but eventually a strong hand will be needed.

As jihad continues to come to Europe's doorstep, Europeans will eventually tire of Muslim terror and the ever-present threat of oil blackmail. What will be the solution? Centralized power in the hands of an oligarchy and, eventually, one man who will enforce peace and keep the Middle Eastern oil flowing. Dictatorship and iron-fisted power is the only form of government that can effectively crush terror. The current governments of Europe are ill-equipped to crush terror and maintain peace. People in Europe will gladly give authority to a ten-leader ruling body, as Daniel 2 and 7 predict, if they can insure continued peace and prosperity.

What we see in Europe right now shows that the main power blocs of the end times are already taking shape. Russia and the Arab/Islamic nations are coming together against Europe and the West. Current events in France are a faint foreshadow of what will continue as the cleavage between East and West continues to grow. The ten-king government of Europe and eventually the rule of Antichrist may not be far behind.

THE MUSLIM CARTOON RIOTS

Flemming Rose, the culture editor of a Danish newspaper, *Jyllands-Posten*, issued a challenge to the editorial cartoonists in his country to see who had the nerve to draw what they thought of the Islamic prophet Muhammad and sign their names. The result of this challenge was twelve caricatures of the prophet ranging from fairly tame representations to some that associated him with Islamic terrorists. In one, he was pictured with a bomb in his turban, brandishing a scimitar, breaking the news to newly arrived martyrs in Paradise that it had run out of virgins.

The cartoons were published by *Jyllands-Posten* on September 30, 2005. In December a complaint was filed in the United Nations by the Organization of the Islamic Conference, which represents fifty-six Muslim states. The complaint alleged human rights violations against Denmark for allowing the publication of the offensive cartoons. Denmark refused to apologize on the basis that it had no jurisdiction over the actions of the newspaper due to freedom of the press. In a show of solidarity with Denmark and freedom of the press, other European newspapers published the cartoons.

As a result, the Islamic world exploded. Boycotts against Denmark rapidly escalated into violent Muslim mobs. Demonstrations in several nations resulted in deaths. Muslim clerics issued *fatwas* calling for the death of the twelve cartoonists, who all went into hiding.

Iran and Syria fanned the flames of fanaticism, inciting payback for the alleged blasphemy. Muslim rage, originally focused on Denmark, quickly expanded to all of Europe and the entire West including, of course, the United States. Protesters called for terrorist attacks against Europe in retaliation.

Protesters in London carried signs and placards that read:
Slay those who insult Islam
Behead those who insult Islam
Exterminate those who slander Islam
Butcher those who mock
Europe will pay
Prepare for the Real Holocaust

In retaliation for the Muhammad cartoons, the Iranian newspaper, *Hamshahri*, initiated an international cartoon contest about the Holocaust. The paper began a contest soliciting Holocaust cartoons offering gold coins to the twelve best artists—the exact same number of cartoons that appeared in the Danish newspaper *Jyllands-Posten*.

By March 2006, Iran's "Holocaust Cartoon Contest" had received entries from 200 people with some drawings mocking the slaughter of Jews by Nazi Germany. One entry allegedly pictured Jews going into a gas pipeline. Most of the contestant entrants were Iranians, but six were from Americans and some were submitted from as far away as Indonesia and Brazil.

In a further act of retaliation, Iran has cut all trade and economic ties with Denmark because of the publication of the satirical cartoons of the Prophet Mohammad that appeared in Danish newspapers.

The clash of civilizations we are witnessing today is much more than just burning cars and blasphemous cartoons. It's a collision of completely different worldviews and cultures. This widening division of the nations into the configuration predicted in the end times is one more indication the coming of Christ could be very soon.

FOLLOWING A SLANDERED SAVIOR

Before we end this chapter, I believe it's important to pause for a moment and reflect on a very important issue. The frenzied reaction of Muslims to the caricatures of Muhammad reveals a great deal about Islam, and especially its stark contrast with biblical Christianity. The clash of civilizations is a clash of worldviews. A clash of values. And ultimately a clash between Muhammad and Christ.

John Piper, a well-known theologian, pastor, and author, made this profound observation in the wake of the Muslim cartoon riots.

We saw last week in the Islamic demonstrations over Danish cartoons of Muhammad another vivid depiction of the difference between Muhammad and Christ, and what it means to follow each. Not all Muslims approve the violence. But a deep lesson remains: The work of Muhammad is based on being honored and the work of Christ is based on being insulted. This produces two very different reactions to mockery.

If Christ had not been insulted, there would be no salvation. This was His saving work: to be insulted and die to rescue sinners from the wrath of God. Already in the Psalms the path of mockery was promised: 'All who see me mock me; they make mouths at me; they wag their heads' (Psalm 22:7). 'He was despised and rejected by men... as one from whom men hide their faces... and we esteemed him not' (Isaiah 53:3).

When it actually happened it was worse than expected. 'They stripped him and put a scarlet robe on him, and twisting together a crown of thorns, they put it on his head.... And kneeling before him, they mocked him, saying, 'Hail, King of the Jews!' And they spit on him' (Matthew 27:28–29). His response to all this was patient endurance. This was the work he came to do. 'Like a lamb that is led to the slaughter, and like a sheep that before its shearers is silent, so he opened not his mouth' (Isaiah 53:7).[74]

Piper then notes how this is *the* crucial distinction between Christ and Muhammad.

That's the most basic difference between Christ and Muhammad and between a Muslim and a follower of Christ. For Christ, enduring the mockery of the cross was the essence of his mission. For a true follower of Christ, enduring suffering patiently for the glory of Christ is the essence of obedience. 'Blessed are you when others revile you and persecute you and utter all kinds of evil against you falsely on my account' (Matthew 5:11). During his life on earth Jesus was called a bastard (John 8:41), a drunkard (Matthew 11:19), a blasphemer (Matthew 26:65), a devil (Matthew 10:25); and he promised his followers the same: 'If they have called the master of the house Beelzebul, how much more will they malign those of his household' (Matthew 10:25).[75]

Muslims are enraged when Muhammad, a man, is insulted or mocked. Yet, Jesus was a man, and very God of very God, who stooped to the lowest low. We should gratefully thank God for a Savior who came to this earth—God in human flesh—who willingly allowed sinful men to hang Him on a cross and mock and revile Him. Jesus suffered and bled and died for the very ones who mocked His glorious name. The just One died in place of the unjust to bring us to God.

Jesus is still being openly mocked and insulted today. And so are His followers. Movies like *The Last Temptation of Christ* and bestselling books like the *Da Vinci Code* blaspheme and demean Christ. While we certainly don't like this, Jesus warned us in advance that it would be this way and commanded us to not retaliate in kind. But it won't be this way forever. Someday Jesus will come back to earth as the Lion of the Tribe of Judah to crush His enemies, deliver His people, and set up His kingdom of righteousness and peace. However, before the real King steps forward, thing are really going to heat up in the Middle East.

CHAPTER 13

RUSSIA, IRAN, AND THE COMING INVASION OF ISRAEL

Great events in history often gather momentum and power long before they are recognized by the experts and commentators on world affairs. Easily one of the most neglected but powerfully galvanizing forces shaping history in the world today is the prophecy of Gog and Magog from the 38th and 39th chapters of the book of Ezekiel.

JON MARK RUTHVEN,
THE PROPHECY THAT IS SHAPING HISTORY

Sometimes listening to the news or reading the newspaper can be like staring at a table covered with pieces of a jigsaw puzzle. There seem to be so many articles and reports that relate to the stage setting for the end times, but sometimes it's difficult to put the pieces together.

What's the key to successfully putting a jigsaw puzzle together? The picture on the box. In the same way, God's prophecies in the Bible serve as the guide, master plan, or picture on the box by which we can evaluate the many current events in our world today to see how they fit together in God's program for this world.

Ezekiel 38–39 is a key part of the picture on the box of God's master plan for history. In this chapter, I want you to join me as we take a serious look at the details of these two chapters in God's Word to see what the picture on the box looks like, and then to evaluate how events in our world today seem to be fitting together to mirror what we see in these chapters.

ANCIENT EZEKIEL AND MODERN IRAN

As we have already seen, the words *Persia*, *Persian*, and *Persians* occur a total of thirty-five times in the Old Testament. Thirty-four of these references clearly refer to the ancient Persian Empire and have, therefore, already been literally fulfilled. However, the reference to Persia in Ezekiel 38:5 is still future in our day. Since the prophecies about ancient Persia have been literally fulfilled, we can rest assured that when the time comes, the prophecy in Ezekiel 38 will be literally fulfilled as well.

Ezekiel 38 describes a great coalition of nations that will invade the land of Israel when Israel is regathered and resting in her land (Ezekiel 38:8, 11, 14).

> "After many days you will be summoned; in the latter years you will come into the land that is restored from the sword, whose inhabitants have been gathered from many nations to the mountains of Israel which had been a continual waste; but its people were brought out from the nations, and they are living securely, all of them…. And you will say, 'I will go up against the land of unwalled villages. I will go against those who are at rest, that live securely, all of them living without walls and having no bars or gates… "Therefore prophesy, son of man, and say to Gog, 'Thus says the Lord GOD, "On that day when My people Israel are living securely, will you not know it?"

One of the specific nations that will participate in this massive military campaign is Persia, or Iran, mentioned in Ezekiel 38:5. It's the easiest of all the nations in Ezekiel 38 to identify. The ancient land of Persia became the modern nation of Iran in March 1935, and then the name was changed to the Islamic Republic of Iran in 1979.

The present military preparations in Iran and the alliances she is forming with her neighbors all point to the literal, impending fulfillment of Ezekiel 38.

Ezekiel 38 predicts a coming Iranian invasion of Israel. However, Iran will not act alone. The prophet Ezekiel wrote these chapters about 2,600 years ago, yet they read like today's headlines. Ezekiel specifically listed the precise alliance of nations that will invade Israel in the latter years, or end times. The list is found in Ezekiel 38:1–6:

And the word of the LORD came to me saying, "Son of man, set your face toward Gog of the land of Magog, the prince of Rosh, Meshech and Tubal, and prophesy against him and say, 'Thus says the Lord GOD, "Behold, I am against you, O Gog, prince of Rosh, Meshech and Tubal. I will turn you about and put hooks into your jaws, and I will bring you out, and all your army, horses and horsemen, all of them splendidly attired, a great company with buckler and shield, all of them wielding swords; Persia, Ethiopia and Put with them, all of them with shield and helmet; Gomer with all its troops; Beth-togarmah from the remote parts of the north with all it troops—many peoples with you."

GOG AND HIS ARMY

The prophecy of the battle of Gog and Magog begins with a list of ten proper names in 38:1–7. The name Gog, which occurs eleven times in Ezekiel 38–39, is a name or title of the leader of the invasion. It is clear that Gog is an individual since he is directly addressed several times by God (38:14; 39:1) and since he is called a prince (38:2; 39:1). It's very important to distinguish Gog from the final world ruler, or Antichrist. Some have erroneously concluded that that Gog is just another name for the Antichrist, but they are not the same person.

Here are the key differences between these two end-time rulers.

GOG	ANTICHRIST
Leads a Russian-Islamic coalition.	Leads a Western coalition and eventually rules the entire world.
Destroyed near the middle of the tribulation.	Destroyed at the end of the tribulation.

The other nine proper names in Ezekiel 38:1–7 are specific geographical locations: Magog, Rosh, Meshech, Tubal, Persia, Cush, Put, Gomer, and Beth-togarmah. All nine of these locations are found in the Table of the Nations in Genesis 10:2–7. The only one that is questionable is Rosh, but it is likely that the name Rosh is actually derived from the name Tiras in Genesis 10:2. [76] It makes sense for Ras or Rosh to be listed in Genesis 10 since all the other nations in Ezekiel 38:1–7 are also listed there.

None of the place names in Ezekiel 38:1–7 exist on any modern map. Ezekiel used ancient place names that were familiar to the people of his day. While the names of these geographical locations have changed many times throughout history and may change again, the geographical territory remains the same. Regardless of what names they may carry at the time of this invasion, it is these specific geographical areas that will be involved.[77] Each of these ancient geographical locations from Ezekiel's day will be briefly examined, and the modern counterpart will be identified.

MEET MAGOG

According to the Jewish historian Josephus, the ancient Scythians inhabited the land of Magog.[78] The Scythians were northern nomadic tribes who inhabited territory from Central Asia across the southern steppes of modern Russia. Magog today probably represents the southern republics or underbelly of the former Soviet Union: Kazakhstan, Kirghizia, Uzebekistan, Turkmenistan, and Tajikistan. Afghanistan could also be part of this territory.

All of these nations are dominated by Islam with a combined total population in excess of sixty million. In 1991–92, Iran began to exert influence in the new governments of Central Asia by initiating diplomatic campaigns in these nations.

ROSH AND RUSSIA

Modern prophecy teachers have often identified Rosh in Ezekiel 38:2 with Russia. However, many have begun to question this identification. Many scholars totally dismiss any notion that the word Rosh in Ezekiel 38–39 could have any possible connection to modern Russia. [79] One argument against identifying Rosh with Russia is that it is "impossibly anachronistic" since the name Russia did not appear until the Middle Ages.[80] Others maintain that those who identify Rosh as Russia base the connection only on the similarity in sound between the two words. However, all competent scholars would agree that one should not equate an English word with a Hebrew word just because the two words sound alike.

The word *Rosh* in Hebrew simply means "head, top, summit, or chief." It is a very common word and is used in all Semitic languages. It occurs over six hundred times in the Old Testament.

Many modern English translations render *Rosh* as a common noun and translate it as the word "chief." The King James Version, Revised Standard Version, English Standard Version, New American Bible and the New International Version all adopt this translation. In Ezekiel 38:2, the NIV reads, "the chief prince of Meshech and Tubal."

However, the Jerusalem Bible, New English Bible, and New American Standard Bible all translate Rosh as a proper name indicating a geographical location. The NASB says, "the prince of Rosh, Meshech, and Tubal." It seems best in light of all the evidence to take Rosh in Ezekiel 38:2 as a proper name of geographical location that existed in Ezekiel's day.[81]

But does Ezekiel's Rosh have any relation to the nation we know today as Russia? There are three reasons for identifying ancient Rosh with modern Russia. The first argument is linguistic. Wilhelm Gesenius, who died in 1842 and is considered by modern Hebrew scholars as one of the greatest scholars of the Hebrew language, unquestionably believed that Rosh in Ezekiel was a proper noun identifying Russia. Gesenius says that "Rosh in Ezek 38:2, 3; 39:1 is a, pr. n. of a northern nation, mentioned with Meshech and Tubal; undoubtedly the *Russians*, who are mentioned by the Byzantine writers of the tenth century, under the name *the Ros*, dwelling to the north of Taurus... as dwelling on the river Rha (*Wolga*)."[82]

Second, there is considerable historical evidence that a place known as Rosh was very familiar in the ancient world. While the word has a variety of forms and spellings, it is clear that the same people are in view. Rosh (*Rash*) is identified as a place that existed as early as 2600 BC in Egyptian inscriptions. There is a later Egyptian inscription from about 1500 B.C that refers to a land called *Reshu* that was located to the north of Egypt.[83]

The place name *Rosh* (or its equivalent in the respective languages) is found at least twenty times in other ancient documents. It is found three times in the Septuagint, which is a Greek translation of the Hebrew Old Testament. It's found ten times in Sargon's inscriptions, once in Assurbanipal's cylinder, once in Sennacherib's annals, and five times in Ugaritic tablets.[84] Rosh was apparently a well-known place in Ezekiel's day. In the sixth century BC, when Ezekiel wrote his prophecy, several bands of the Rosh people lived in an area to the north of the Black Sea.

After providing extensive evidence of the origin and early history of the Rosh people, and then tracing them through the centuries, Clyde Billington concluded:

Historical, ethnological, and archaeological evidence all favor the conclusion that the Rosh people of Ezekiel

38–39 were the ancestors of the Rus/Ros people of Europe and Asia.... The Rosh people who are mentioned in Ezekiel 38–39 were well-known to ancient and medieval writers by a variety of names which all derived from the names of Tiras and Rosh.... Those Rosh people who lived to the north of the Black Sea in ancient and medieval times were called the Rus/Ros/Rox/Aorsi from very early times.... From this mixture with Slavs and with the Varangian Rus in the 9th century, the Rosh people of the area north of the Black Sea formed the people known today as the Russians.[85]

The third reason is geographical. Ezekiel says several times that the invading force that comes into Israel comes from "the remote parts of the north" (38:6,15) and "the remotest parts of the north" (39:2). Directions in the Bible are always in relation to Israel, which is the center of the earth according to Ezekiel 38:12. If you look at a world map, you will find that Russia is directly north and northeast of Israel. When you draw a line north of Israel and keep going to the "remote" and "remotest" parts of the north, you end up in Russia. The only thing farther north of Russia is the Arctic Ocean and the icebergs.

Therefore, for these three reasons, I believe that Russia will be an integral part of the end-time strike force that comes against Israel.

Many have thought that the fall of the Soviet Union in the early 1990s totally eliminated Russia from the prophetic picture. However, the fall of the Soviet Union and the rise of the independent Muslim republics that were part of the former Soviet empire may actually give Russia a stronger alliance and stake in Islamic affairs. Back on May 21, 1993, the *Jerusalem Post* made this prediction:

> What the West seems to have forgotten is that Russian interest in the Middle East precedes the advent of communism. It is not about to disappear with the demise of the Soviet Empire. In fact, Russia has certain advantages in the regional power play. Communism's sweet promise may have lost its appeal for the region's oppressed peoples. But the rise of independent Islamic republics within the Russian orbit may become a far more effective weapon in the battle for their hearts and minds.

MESHECH AND TUBAL

Students of Bible prophecy in the past consistently identified Meshech and Tubal with the Russian cities of Moscow and Tobolsk. However, this identification is based on similarity of sound and pronunciation rather than solid historical evidence. Meshech and Tubal are identified in ancient history with the Mushki and Tabal of the Assyrians, and the Moschi and Tibareni of the Greeks who inhabited territory that is in the modern nation of Turkey. At every point in the history of these two nations, they occupied territory that is presently in the modern nation of Turkey.

CUSH

The Hebrew word *Cush* in Ezekiel 38:5 is often translated "Ethiopia" in modern versions. Secular history locates Cush directly south of ancient Egypt extending down past the modern city of Khartoum, which is the capital of modern Sudan.[86] Thus, modern Sudan inhabits the ancient land of Cush. Sudan is a hard-line Islamic nation that supported Iraq in the Gulf War and harbored Osama bin Laden from 1991 to 1996. The National Islamic Front which is headquartered in Khartoum is part of the world-terror network.

Iran and Sudan are mentioned side-by-side in Ezekiel 38:5, and they are strong allies today. Beginning in 1991–92 Iran began to aggressively deepen her ties with the new Sudanese government. Kenneth Pollack points out the close connection between Iran and Sudan. "They quickly deepened their ties with the new Sudanese government. Tehran and Khartoum exchanged high-level visits, signed trade deals, and crafted an agreement on military cooperation, while Iran sent military and intelligence advisers from the Revolutionary Guard to Sudan."[87]

Ezekiel's alliance of nations is coming together.

PUT

It's clear from ancient sources that *Put* or *Phut* was a North African nation (Jeremiah 46:9; Ezekiel 27:10; 30:5; Nahum 3:9). From the ancient *Babylon Chronicle* it appears that *Putu* was the "distant" land to the west of Egypt, which would be modern day Libya.[88] The Septuagint renders the word *Put* as *Libues*. *The Brown-Driver-Briggs Lexicon* Hebrew lexicon also identifies Put with Libya.[89] Modern Libya, which is an Islamic nation, has been under the rule of Colonel Mu'ammar al-Gadhafi since 1969.

GOMER

It was very popular a few decades ago, during the Cold War, to identify Gomer with East Germany. Gomer is probably a reference to the ancient Cimmerians or *Kimmerioi*. *The Cambridge Ancient History* states that the Assyrian *Gimirai* is the Hebrew *Gomer*.[90] Beginning in the eighth century BC the Cimmerians occupied territory in Anatolia, which is modern Turkey.[91] Josephus noted that the Gomerites were identified with the Galatians who inhabited what today is central Turkey.[92]

BETH-TOGARMAH

The Hebrew word "beth" means "house," so Beth-togarmah means the "house of Togarmah." Beth-togarmah is mentioned in Ezekiel 27:14 as a nation that traded horses and mules with ancient Tyre. Ezekiel 38:6 states that Beth-togarmah comes from "the remote parts of the north with all its troops." Ancient Togarmah was also known as Til-garamu (Assyrian) or Tegarma (Hittite) and its territory is in modern Turkey, which is north of Israel.

Turkey is presently seeking admittance to the European Union. From every indication, it appears that Turkey's request for admission will be denied. When Turkey is officially rebuffed and denied entrance the to the EU, most experts agree that she will turn back to the east to secure her geopolitical interests. This will push her into the waiting arms of Iran and Russia, and the Gog coalition will be ready to strike.

NAMING THE NATIONS

With these identifications in mind, it's now possible to put the invading strike force together and see the entire picture.

THE INVADERS IN EZEKIEL 38–39

ANCIENT NAME	MODERN NAME
Rosh (Rashu, Rasapu, Ros, and Rus)	Russia
Magog (Scythians)	Central Asia and possibly Afghanistan
Meshech (Muschki and Musku)	Turkey
Tubal (Tubalu)	Turkey
Persia	Iran
Ethiopia (Cush)	Sudan
Put or Phut	Libya
Gomer (Cimmerians)	Turkey
Beth-togarmah (Til-garimmu or Tegarma)	Turkey

WHERE'S IRAQ IN ALL THIS?

All of this raises a very important question for anyone who has studied Bible prophecy. *Why doesn't Iraq (ancient Babylon) join the Islamic confederation of nations when they invade Israel in the end times?* As you read the list of nations that will invade Israel in the end times, one nation is conspicuous by its absence. Turkey is mentioned, along with Iran, the Islamic nations of Central Asia, Russia, Sudan, and Libya. But where is Iraq? Where is Babylon? Why is Iraq missing from this list? After all, Iraq would love to invade, plunder, and annihilate Israel just as much as any other Islamic state.

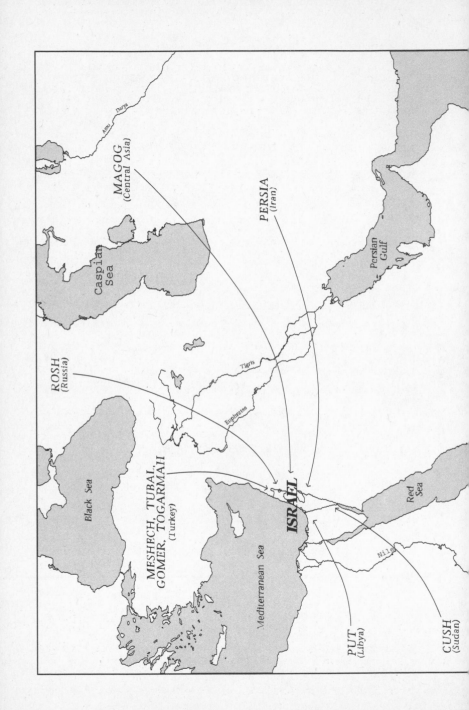

I believe Iraq's absence from this invasion is quite clear if we follow God's blueprint for the end times, in Scripture.

First of all, I believe that the ancient city of Babylon will be rebuilt in the end times as a great commercial capital for the Antichrist (see Isaiah 13; Revelation 17–18). This means that the current war in Iraq, that presently has no end in sight, must end at some point. This is great news for all Americans. The war has dragged on for over three years, and as of April 2006 the American death toll stood at almost 2,400. For a great European leader to build a headquarters in Babylon will require some degree of stability in Iraq. This great leader, also known as the Antichrist, will make a seven-year peace pact with Israel according to Daniel 9:27. The signing of this covenant is actually the event that begins the seven-year Tribulation period. If the Antichrist has his commercial, eastern capital in Babylon, then it's not hard to figure out why Iraq will not join the rest of these Muslim nations when they invade Israel just before the middle of the seven-year Tribulation. Babylon will be controlled by the Antichrist, the leader of the Western world, who signed the peace treaty with Israel. If this scenario is correct, it means that at some point in the future, Europe will begin to exert more influence in Iraq. With the protracted quagmire in Iraq, this notion is not far-fetched. It makes sense that at some point down the line, Europe may try to come to Iraq's rescue. This would fit in with Europe's newly assumed role as the world's peacemaker.

Second, the Bible says that Babylon will be destroyed at the end of the Tribulation just before Jesus comes back to earth. According to Ezekiel 38, the Islamic invaders will be destroyed in the first half of the Tribulation. The omission of Babylon from Ezekiel 38 is consistent with God's predictions elsewhere about her destiny. She will not meet her doom with the other Islamic nations during the Tribulation, but will be destroyed later. Babylon has her own personal appointment with destiny just before the Second Coming of Christ.

IRAN'S FINAL JIHAD

When Iran and her allies decide to invade Israel, there will be no stopping them. They will be bent on war and destruction. It will look like the perfect time, and they will not back down.

When these nations invade the land of Israel, it will look like the biggest mismatch in history. It will make the invasions of Israel in 1967 and 1973 by Arab nations pale in comparison. When the leader of this army assembles this last-days strike force, it will look like Israel is finished. Israel will be completely surrounded. This time, the Jewish people will not be able to overcome their enemies by their own strength and ingenuity. Israel will be totally overwhelmed. Gog and his army will cover Israel like a cloud. However, the Bible says that God will come to the rescue of His people. Almighty God will intervene to win the battle for His people. Ezekiel 38–39 describes what we might call the "One-Day War" or even the "One-Hour War" because God will quickly, completely annihilate the Islamic invaders from the face of the earth by supernatural means.

Here's how Ezekiel graphically describes it.

"It will come about on that day, when Gog comes against the land of Israel," declares the Lord GOD, "that My fury will mount up in My anger. In my zeal and in My blazing wrath I declare that on that day there will surely be a great earthquake in the land of Israel. The fish of the sea, the birds of the heavens, the beasts of the field, all the creeping things that creep on the earth, and all the men who are on the face of the earth will shake at My presence; the mountains also will be thrown down, the steep pathways will collapse, and every wall will fall to the ground. I will call for a sword against him on all My mountains," declares the Lord God. "Every man's sword will be against his brother. With pestilence and with blood I shall enter into judgment with him; and I shall rain on him, and on his troops, and on the many peoples who are with him, a torrential rain, with hailstones, fire and brimstone. I shall magnify Myself, sanctify Myself, and make Myself known in the sight of many nations; and they will know that I am the LORD." (38:18–23)

God will mount up in His fury to destroy these godless invaders. God will come to rescue his helpless people using four means to totally destroy Russia and her Islamic allies.[93]

1. A great earthquake (38:19–20). According to Jesus, the coming tribulation will be a time of many terrible earthquakes (Matthew 24:7). But this specific earthquake will be used by God to conquer and confuse these invaders.

2. Infighting among the troops of the various nations (38:21). In the chaos after the powerful earthquake, the armies of each of the nations represented will turn against each other. Just think about it: the troops from the various invading nations will speak Russian, Farsi (Persian), Arabic, and Turkic languages. They will

probably begin to kill anyone that they can't identify. This could be the largest case of death by friendly fire in human history.

3. Disease (38:22a). Gog and his troops will experience a horrible, lethal plague that will add to the misery and devastation already inflicted.

4. Torrential rain, hailstones, fire, and burning sulphur (38:22b). Just as God destroyed Sodom and Gomorrah, He will pour fire from heaven on the invading army.

These nations will arrogantly, boldly swoop down on Israel to take her land, but the only piece of land they will claim in Israel will be their burial plots (Ezekiel 39:12). They will set out to bury Israel, but God will bury them.

At a meeting in April 2006 in support of the Palestinians, the Iranian President made some incredible comments that point toward the fulfillment of Ezekiel 38–39. He said that Palestine "will soon be freed." He called Israel a "constant threat" and "permanent threat to the Middle East" and said the Middle East will "soon be liberated." Did you notice the use of the word "soon"? He also said that Israel is "heading towards annihilation." In one of his most shocking statements, the Iranian President said, "The Zionist regime is a rotten, dried tree that will be eliminated by one storm." This sounds like an open threat of a nuclear attack against Israel. What other storm could eliminate the entire nation?

Ahmadinejad's statements are chilling in light of Ezekiel 38:9 which describes the future invasion of Israel. "And you will go up, you will come like a *storm*, you will be like a *cloud* covering the land, you and all your troops, and many peoples with you." Ezekiel 38:16 says, "and you will come up against

My people Israel like a *cloud* to cover the land. It shall come about in the last days." Ahmadinejad is using language straight from Ezekiel 38 to describe his evil intentions toward Israel.

ISLAM'S VERSION OF EZEKIEL 38–39

Ironically, Islam has its own version of the Battle of Gog and Magog called the War of Yajuj and Majuj, but it's very different from the biblical account.

In two places the Koran specifically mentions "Gog and Magog" (Yajuj and Majuj) by name (18:96; 21:96). Islamic eschatology teaches that there are ten major signs that signal the approach of the end and the day of resurrection. There are various opinions about the order of these signs, but in at least one list Gog and Magog is the number four sign.

According to Islamic teaching, Gog and Magog are two groups of Turks that were spreading corruption through the earth during the time of Abraham. Finally, to keep them in check, they were enclosed behind a great barrier. They tried in vain to climb over it and have been trying to dig under the wall for centuries, but they will not be able to get out until Allah decrees that they can be released. Then, the barrier will collapse, and Gog and Magog will pour out in all directions rushing into the land of Israel to attack the Muslims there. When Jesus prays against Gog and Magog, Allah will wipe them out by means of some kind of disease or plague that he will send upon them. The disease is described as either infectious, lethal boils, or a disease that eats the flesh from their bones.

If that sounds familiar, it should. It was evidently taken by Muhammad straight from Ezekiel 38 with a few convenient changes to fit his own ends. Ezekiel 38:22 specifically says that

God will destroy the invaders with disease and with blood. Therefore, while Muslims believe in the prophecy of Gog and Magog, they appear to be totally ignorant of the fact that all the nations in Ezekiel 38 that will be destroyed by God are Muslim nations today, with the exception of Russia. One of their ten great signs of the end will actually be fulfilled by them when they attack Israel in the last days.

GOD IS IN CONTROL

At the end of every movie when the credits begin to run one of the first items to appear is "directed by..." If Bible prophecy had a list of credits, it would read, "directed by God." God is not only the author of the script, He is the producer and director as well. He is orchestrating, organizing, and overruling world events to set the stage so that all the props and players will be in the right place when the curtain goes up at the Rapture. Over and over again in Ezekiel 38–39 God makes it clear that He is in charge, that He's the director. If there's one thing we learn from Ezekiel 38–39 above all else, it's that God is in control.

He says to these future invaders, "And I will turn you about, and put hooks into your jaws, and I will bring you out" (38:4). God pictures these invading nations as a huge crocodile that he drags out of the water.

Seven times in Ezekiel 38–39 we read the same words, "Thus says the Lord God" (38:2,10,14,17; 39:1,17,25). Another eight times the refrain, "declares the Lord God," appears. Obviously, God doesn't want us to miss the point—this is His Word. The prediction in Ezekiel 38–39 comes directly from Him. He is the author of the script.

In other places, God further emphasizes that He is sovereignly at work in human affairs. "You will be summoned" (38:8), "I shall bring you against My land" (38:16), "and I shall turn you around, drive you on, take you up… and bring you against the mountains of Israel" (39:2). Obviously, God is not violating the will of these invaders by bringing them into Israel. They want to come. They "devise an evil plan," and God holds them responsible for it (38:10). Nothing in this statement is meant in any way to lessen human responsibility. The point is that God is ultimately and finally in control. He's the director. He is the one who is making sure the stage is perfectly set for His great prophetic production.

There are many events and participants that God has scripted to play a role in His prophetic production, but as we have seen, one of the major events that God has scripted for the end times is the Battle of Gog and Magog. The first great military campaign of the coming tribulation.

While the rise of militant Islam has shocked and surprised most people, amazingly, 2,600 years ago, God, through the prophet Ezekiel, predicted the exact scenario that we see developing before our eyes every day on the evening news.

Ezekiel 36–39 is "history written beforehand." Ezekiel 36–37 describes the regathering of Jews to the land of Israel in the end times. In Ezekiel 38–39 this regathering is followed by an all-out invasion of Israel by a massive assault force. On May 14, 1948, Israel became a nation against all odds, preparing the way for the first part of Ezekiel's prophecy to be fulfilled. As we look around today, it appears that the stage is being set for the rest of his prophecy to come to pass exactly as God predicted.

CENTER STAGE

God's Word is clear that Iran still occupies a place in God's prophetic program. Ezekiel 38 names Iran as one of the chief participants in the Islamic confederation of nations that will invade regathered, resting Israel in the last days. Iran is arming herself militarily in an unparalleled fashion and is fomenting disdain and hatred for Israel and the West. And, amazingly, at the same time, we see the coalition described in Ezekiel 38 forming today. Iran is developing close ties to Russia, the Muslim nations of Central Asia, and Sudan.

Iran's invasion of Israel seems to be on the horizon, but how soon will it take place? How close are we? When will Iran and her allies invade Israel?

CHAPTER 14

WHEN WILL IRAN INVADE ISRAEL?

Ezekiel's prophecy obviously could not have been fulfilled prior to 1945, for the nation of Israel was not regathered to their ancient land. Until our generation, Israel's situation did not correspond to that which is described in Ezekiel's passage.

JOHN WALVOORD, *THE NATIONS IN PROPHECY*

God's Word indicates that Iran, along with Russia and a vast horde of Muslim allies, will invade the land of Israel in the last days. It is not a question of *whether* these events will be fulfilled, but rather *when*. Ezekiel plainly says over and over again that his message is a message from Almighty God. Therefore, the prophecy of Ezekiel 38–39 *will be fulfilled* exactly as God has said.

Iran and her allies will invade Israel in the last days!

As we scan the horizon, it appears that the final showdown between Israel, Iran, and the other Muslim nations could be very near. But how near?

When does the Bible say this clash will occur? When is this event scheduled on God's timetable of events? What events are necessary to set the stage for this colossal offensive?

Let's see what the Bible says about the timing of this important end-time event.

THE GENERAL IDENTIFICATION OF THE TIME

By far, the most controversial issue in Ezekiel 38–39 is the setting or timing of the invasion. The specific time of the invasion in Ezekiel 38 is difficult to determine. Concerning this issue, one would be wise to follow the advice of Clarence E. Mason. "One thing is certain; no teacher should speak dogmatically on a prophecy like that of Gog and Magog in Ezekiel 38–39. So many different views have been offered that it is difficult to sift, discard, and retain.... It is the details, particularly as to the time of the action, regarding which there is disagreement."[94]

While the specific time is harder to pin down, the general identification can be ascertained with certainty. While some believe that the events in Ezekiel 38–39 have already occurred, the vast majority of Bible scholars agree that this invasion has not been fulfilled in the past, but wholly awaits a future fulfillment.[95] Three main factors support this conclusion.

First, in Ezekiel 38:8, the prophet says specifically that this invasion will occur in the "latter years." This is the only occurrence of this exact phrase in the Old Testament. Another similar phrase occurs a few verses later in Ezekiel 38:16. "It shall come about in *the last days* that I shall bring you against My land" . This phrase is used in the Old Testament in reference to Israel's final time of distress or to Israel's final restoration to the Messianic kingdom (Isaiah 2:2; Jeremiah 23:20; 30:24; Hosea 3:5; Micah 4:1). Likewise, in Ezekiel 38:16, the phrase "in the last days" is a technical term that refers to the end times.[96] Therefore, Ezekiel is telling us that this invasion will occur in the final time of history in preparation for the establishment of the Messianic Kingdom of Christ.

Second, although the land of Israel has been the scene of countless battles, wars, and invasions, nothing even remotely similar to the events in Ezekiel 38–39 has ever occurred in the past. When has Israel ever been invaded by all these nations listed in Ezekiel 38:1–6? Or when did God ever destroy an invading army like this with fire and brimstone from heaven, plagues, earthquakes, and infighting among the invaders (Ezekiel 38:19–22). The answer? Never. That is because Ezekiel is describing an invasion that is still in the future, even in our day. If one believes that the Bible is God's Word, that it's infallible, and that it must be literally fulfilled, then the only logical conclusion is that Ezekiel describes an end-time invasion of Israel.[97]

Third, the setting of these chapters is important. Ezekiel 33–39 is one of four main divisions in this book, and this section deals with Israel's future restoration. Chapter 37 deals with Israel's restoration to the land; however, the initial regathering is in unbelief. Chapter 40 begins a new section describing the millennial temple and sacrifices. Therefore, the invasion of Gog and Magog is placed sometime between the beginning of Israel's restoration to the land and the beginning of the Millennium or 1,000-year earthly reign of Christ.

The modern restoration of Israel to her land began in the late 1800s, but the key date was 1948 when the modern nation was officially born. With Israel restored as a nation in 1948, the first necessary precondition for the fulfillment of Ezekiel 38–39 moved strategically into place. Because, obviously, the nation of Israel can't be invaded if she doesn't exist.

NARROWING IT DOWN

It's clear that Ezekiel 38–39 is describing a future, end-time invasion of Israel by Iran and her allies, but is it possible to narrow the time down any further? Are there any clues as to the specific time? How close could it be?

COULD IT HAPPEN BEFORE THE RAPTURE?

The popular *Left Behind* series places this invasion of Israel at the very beginning of the great events of the end times, even before the Rapture occurs. The following is an excerpt from the opening scenes of *Left Behind.*

> Frustrated at their inability to profit from Israel's fortune and determined to dominate and occupy the Holy Land, the Russians had launched an attack against Israel in the middle of the night. The assault became known as the Russian Pearl Harbor... The number of aircraft and warheads made it clear their mission was annihilation....
>
> Miraculously, not one casualty was reported in all of Israel. Otherwise Buck might have believed some mysterious malfunction had caused missile and plane to destroy each other. But witnesses reported that it had been a firestorm, along with rain and hail and an earthquake, that consumed the entire offensive effort....
>
> Editors and readers had their own explanations for the phenomenon, but Buck admitted, if only to himself, that he became a believer in God that day. Jewish scholars pointed out passages from the Bible that

talked about God destroying Israel's enemies with a firestorm, earthquake, hail, and rain. Buck was stunned when he read Ezekiel 38 and 39 about a great enemy from the north invading Israel with the help of Persia, Libya, and Ethiopia.[98]

This view has two main strengths. First, it fits well with the seven years for burning the weapons and seven months to bury the dead in Ezekiel 39:9–12. Under this view, the seven years in Ezekiel 39:9 corresponds with the seven-year period ("one week") in Daniel 9:27. This verse says that the Antichrist will make a treaty with Israel for a period of "one week," or one set of seven. In the context of Daniel 9:1–2 and 9:24–26 this set of seven is a reference to seven years. This seven-year period will be the final years of this present age. If the Gog invasion occurs before the Rapture, the seven-year periods in Ezekiel 39:9 and Daniel 9:27 would parallel one another.

Second, this view provides a reasonable explanation for how the Jewish people will be able to construct a temple on the temple mount in Jerusalem. If the armies of many of the major Islamic nations are decimated in Israel before the tribulation begins, the rebuilding of the temple in Jerusalem could be accomplished with much less Muslim resistance.

This view has two main weaknesses. First, according to Ezekiel 38:8 and 16 the invasion will occur in the "latter years" or "last days." As noted above, these expressions appear to refer to the final time of Israel's distress and restoration, or the end times. These chronological indicators point to a time period after the beginning of the tribulation, rather than a time within the church age or during the time between the Rapture and the beginning of the tribulation.

Second, the invasion will occur at a time when Israel is "at rest," "living securely," and dwelling in "unwalled villages." It is true that the inhabitants of modern Israel live in unwalled villages and have some degree of security due to their military might. However, they are not "at rest" as required by Ezekiel 38:11. The Hebrew word translated *at rest* means "be quiet, undisturbed."[99] This hardly describes Israel today. The nation is one huge, armed camp.[100] The people are disturbed on a regular basis by threats and homicide bombings. Since 1948, Israel has lived under the constant threat of terrorist attacks and invasion by her neighbors. The terminology in Ezekiel 38 fits much better with the first half of the seven-year tribulation when Israel will enjoy the protection of her covenant with the Antichrist and will temporarily let down her guard (Daniel 9:27).

IS EZEKIEL DESCRIBING ARMAGEDDON?

Several well-known commentators and prophecy teachers view the battle of Gog and Magog in conjunction with the campaign, or war, of Armageddon at the end of the tribulation. The word *Armageddon* is made up of two Hebrew words: *Har* ("mountain") and *Megiddo* (a city in the northern part of Israel). Megiddo was built on a hill, so the hill was called the mountain (*har*) of Megiddo—or Armageddon. Armageddon is only found in the Bible in Revelation 16:16 and refers to the final great war of this age.

There are two main reasons for equating the battle of Gog and Magog with the war of Armageddon. First, the invitation in Ezekiel 39:4 and 39:17–20 for the birds and beasts to feed on the carnage after the battle of Gog and Magog seems to parallel the description of the great supper after Armageddon in Revelation 19:17–18. You might want to stop and read these passages in your Bible to see how similar they are.

Second, this view dovetails nicely with the statements about Israel's salvation after the invasion since, according to Zechariah 12:10, Israel will turn to the Lord en masse at the end of the tribulation. Ezekiel 39:22 and 29 say, "'And the house of Israel will know that I am the Lord their God from that day onward.... I will not hide My face from them any longer, for I will have poured out My Spirit on the house of Israel,' declares the Lord."

However, there are four main obstacles to this view. First, Ezekiel 38 names specific allies, whereas Armageddon involves all the nations of the earth. Second, in Ezekiel 39 the destruction is on the mountains of Israel while at Armageddon it stretches from Megiddo in the north to Petra in the south. Third, in Ezekiel the armies are destroyed by convulsions of nature, but at Armageddon they are destroyed by the personal appearance of Christ. Fourth, and most importantly, at the end of the tribulation Israel will not be "at rest" or "living securely" which is required by Ezekiel 38:8,11,14. In the time of great tribulation, Israel will not be at rest, for Christ told them to flee to the mountains to escape their persecutors. By the end of the tribulation many Jews will have obeyed Him and fled into the wilderness, and the rest of the Jewish people will have endured three and a half years of persecution by the Antichrist. The end of the tribulation will be one time when Israel will not be "at rest" or "living securely." Therefore, the invasion described by Ezekiel could not be a part of the battle of Armageddon, or the battle of the Great Day of God Almighty.

DIFFERENCES BETWEEN TWO END TIMES WARS

BATTLE OF GOG AND MAGOG (EZEKIEL 38–39)	ARMAGEDDON (REVELATION 16 AND 19)
Gog leads the invasion.	Antichrist leads the invasion.
Israel is at peace.	Israel it not at peace.
Armies gather to plunder Israel.	Armies gather to fight Christ.
Iran, Russia, and Islamic allies invade Israel.	All nations invade Israel.

DURING THE FIRST HALF OF THE TRIBULATION

All things considered, the best view of the time of this massive invasion of Israel is during the first half of the coming seven-year tribulation. There are two main strengths of this view.

First, it provides an excellent explanation for Israel's peace and security described in Ezekiel 38:8 and 11.

As prophecy expert John Walvoord states:

One of the principal questions one could ask about this battle is, When is the battle going to occur? It has not occurred in the past. What indication do we have in this portion of Scripture that the battle will occur at a specific time... One point at which Israel will be at rest is in the millennial kingdom. But we are told expressly that, in the millennial kingdom, there will be no war (Isaiah 2:4), and only when the rebellion occurs at the end of the millennium when Satan is let loose (Revelation 20:7–9) does war break out. Certainly Israel is not going to be at rest under these circumstances either, once Satan is let loose.

There is only one period in the future that clearly fits this description of Ezekiel, and that is the first half of Daniel's seventieth week of God's program for Israel (Daniel 9:27). After the church has been Raptured and saints have been raised from the dead and the living saints have been caught up to be with the Lord, a confederacy of nations will emerge in the Mediterranean Sea. Out of that confederacy will come a strong man who will become its dictator (discussed in previous chapters). He is described in Daniel 9:26 as "the prince that shall come." He will enter into a seven-year covenant of protection and peace with the people of Israel (Daniel 9:27).

Under that covenant, Israel will be able to relax, for their Gentile enemies will have become their friends, apparently guaranteed their borders, and promised them freedom. During that first three and one-half years, we have the one time when regathered Israel is at rest and secure. Apparently Russia will invade the land of Israel during that period, possibly toward its close, and the Scripture will then be fulfilled. [101]

Second, this view provides a reasonable scenario for the Antichrist's ascent to world domination at the mid-point of the tribulation. If the armies of Russia and her Islamic allies are wiped out in Israel some time before the mid-point of the tribulation, this would create a massive power vacuum and a dramatic shift in the balance of power that would allow the Antichrist to ascend to world domination as predicted in Revelation 13.

While no view of the timing of Ezekiel 38–39 is without difficulty, the best view is that the invasion will occur during the first half of the tribulation when Israel has her guard down due to her peace treaty with the Antichrist (Daniel 9:27). This force of nations that hate Israel will seize their opportunity to try to wipe her off the map.

WHAT ABOUT THE WEAPONS AND HORSES?

One issue that you may be wondering about as you read Ezekiel 38–39 is the nature of the weapons and the means of transportation. The weapons mentioned in Ezekiel 38–39 are ancient weapons that are made out of wood such as bows, arrows, shields, war clubs, and spears (39:9), and the means of transportation for the invaders is horses (38:15). How do we account for these ancient weapons if this invasion is in the end times?

There are two main views. First, it is possible that due to some form of disarmament the nations will resort to primitive weapons that can be constructed secretly and easily if a surprise attack were to be successfully achieved.[102] Second, the ancient weapons mentioned could be understood as their modern counterparts. While no view of the nature of the weapons is without problems, this is probably the best view. Ezekiel, inspired by the Holy Spirit, spoke in language that the people of that day could understand. If he had spoken of planes, missiles, tanks, and rifles, this text would have been nonsensical to everyone until the twentieth century. Moreover, the main point of Ezekiel's great prophecy is that a specific group of nations will attack Israel intent on completely destroying her.

The focus clearly is not the specific weapons that will be used by these invaders. Ezekiel communicates in the only way that he can, the powerful and well-equipped nature of the invaders.[103]

This "modernizing" of the weapons is not spiritualizing the text but rather understanding God's Word in its historical context in light of the original audience. The Holy Spirit speaks to people in their own context and culture in ways that communicate God's truth in a meaningful, understandable way.

As noted earlier, nine specific ancient nations are mentioned in Ezekiel 38:1–6. Just as with the weapons, these exact nations, under these specific ancient names, will not attack Israel because they no longer exist under the names in Ezekiel 38. Obviously, there is no Rosh, Gomer, Magog, Meshech, Togarmah, Persia, or Put today on any world map. The names of some of these areas have changed numerous times through the millennia. But the modern nations that inhabit the same geographical territory as the ancient nations will invade Israel. Again, the Holy Spirit speaks to people in language they can grasp. He used the ancient names of these places, going all the way back to Genesis 10 to clearly identify the geographical areas that will invade Israel in the end times.

HOW CLOSE ARE WE?

Events in our world today point toward the impending fulfillment of the battle of Gog and Magog and Iran's invasion of Israel as recorded in Ezekiel 38–39. All of the necessary antecedents for the fulfillment of this prophecy are in place or are moving in that direction.

1. *Israel must be a nation that can be invaded.* This is already in place. It has been since the late 1940s. In fact, in 2006, for the first time since AD 135, there will be more Jews in Israel than in any other place in the world.

2. *Israel must be living in peace and prosperity.* The ongoing peace process between Israel and the Palestinians points toward the coming of the Antichrist who will rise from Europe and finally bring peace and resolve this previously unsolvable issue.

3. *The nations listed in Ezekiel 38 must have the desire and means to invade Israel.* Every nation listed by Ezekiel other than Russia is an Islamic nation and hates Israel with a passion. If Israel were to take out the Iranian nuclear plants in the near future, this would plant seeds of hatred against Israel that could easily precipitate such an invasion in the very near future. At the same time, Russia is rapidly returning to her totalitarian ways, is developing deeper ties with Iran, and is increasing her influence in the Muslim world. This could be the hooks in her jaws.

In his commentary on Ezekiel, published back in 1987, W. A. Criswell, a well-known pastor, wrote these timely words concerning the prophecy of Ezekiel 38–39:

The prophet Ezekiel lived 2,500 years ago, and yet he writes as though he were a correspondent for the daily newspapers of the earth. What he says is so pertinent this moment that it is as though he lived in the places where history is unfolding before our very eyes.[104]

John Walvoord also notes the significance of Ezekiel's prophecy for today.

In the present world scene there are many indications pointing to the conclusion that the end of the age may soon be upon us. These prophecies relating to Israel's coming day of suffering and ultimate restoration may be destined for fulfillment in the present generation. Never before in the history of the world has there been a confluence of major evidences of preparation for the end.

Today, to the north of the nation Israel is the armed might of Russia. Never before has it seemed more likely that the prediction will be fulfilled given by Ezekiel (chapters 38 and 39) of an invasion from the north.[105]

The prelude seems to be in place. All that remains is for the Rapture to take place.

The Rapture could happen at any moment, setting these events on fast forward.

A well-known preacher once said that we should study with our Bible in one hand and the newspaper in the other. This has never been more true or more necessary. Anyone who reads today's headlines in light of God's Word will see ominous developments that may lead to the final great struggle.

We have looked at Ezekiel 38–39 and how world events, especially in Iran, seem to be moving toward the fulfillment of this ancient prophecy. Let's pull all the pieces together now and answer a question that many people are asking—what's next?

CHAPTER 15

WHAT'S NEXT?

17 percent of Americans believe that the end of the world will occur in their lifetime.

DAVID GATES,
NEWSWEEK POLL

Our world today is like a vast stage being set for a great drama. There's every indication that in our own day we are seeing the major end-time players take their places for their future roles during the tribulation. It looks like the curtain could go up at any moment. The Middle East is the world's number one crisis today, occupying the attention of world leaders. The world recognizes the political and economic power in the hands of those who control the tremendous oil reserves of the Middle East. The threat of jihadist terror reverberates from its Middle Easter epicenter. For the foreseeable future, the Middle East will continue to be the focal point of international relationships.

All the necessary historical developments have already taken place. Israel and the nations of the world have been prepared for the final drama. Most important, Israel is regathered back in the land, organized as a nation, and ready for her role in the end times. Today, Israel desperately needs the peace treaty promised in prophecy. Primarily because of the unreasonable demands of the Palestinians, Israel will not be able to attain a satisfactory settlement in direct negotiations.

At the same time, Russia stands poised to the north of Israel for entry in the end-time conflict. The great northern bear is moving back to her totalitarian ways and is strategically positioning herself to increase her power and influence in the Middle East.

Iran is the number one terrorist nation in the world today and appears poised to become an Islamic superpower. As Iran chases nuclear energy, the entire world is holding its collective breath, wondering if we're headed for the nightmare of nuclear jihad. Libya and Sudan are radical Islamic countries who have not abandoned their desire to attack Israel from the south and west. Turkey also appears to be moving into place. Each nation is prepared to play out its role in the final hours of history. [106]

In 1974, John Walvoord, in his best-selling book, *Armageddon, Oil and the Middle East Crisis*, wrote these classic words that are more timely today than when he wrote them.

> Our present world is well prepared for the beginning of the prophetic drama that will lead to Armageddon. Since the stage is being set for this dramatic climax of the age, it must mean that Christ's coming for His own is very near. If there ever was an hour when men should consider their personal relationship to Jesus Christ, it is today. God is saying to this generation: "Prepare for the coming of the Lord."[107]

I couldn't agree more. God's Word for this generation is clear—prepare for the coming of the Lord. Never before in human history has there been such a convergence of trends and developments that are part of the matrix of end-time events predicted in Scripture. And never before have world events had such an immediate, instantaneous impact. Events that decades ago would have taken months or even years to bring about change, now take minutes. This incredible acceleration of impact and effect creates a sense in all of us that we are moving toward a great crisis.

But what should we expect? What's the prophetic forecast look like? What's next?

FUTURE TENSE

From my study of Bible prophecy, here's my best effort at this time to put the pieces together. Here's a sequence of ten key events that I see looming on the horizon.

1. World tensions will continue to build. Israel, Islam, terror, the threat of nuclear jihad, and oil will dominate world news, riveting world focus on the Middle East. The worldwide cry for peace, security, and stability will reach a crescendo.

2. Jesus will come suddenly and without warning to Rapture His bride to heaven. All believers in Christ will be whisked away to the Father's House in heaven. All unbelievers will be left behind.

3. The United States will be greatly affected by the Rapture, losing 30–60 million of its citizens. In the wake of the Rapture and its devastating results on the U.S. economy, there will be a shift of world power away from the U.S. to Europe and Asia.

4. Out of the chaos and confusion created by the Rapture, the Antichrist will rise from a reunited form of the Roman Empire led by an oligarchy or ruling

committee consisting of ten leaders. This revived or reunited Roman Empire will probably be some future form of the European Union. This final Roman prince will make a seven-year peace treaty with Israel, ushering in a brief season of worldwide peace (Daniel 9:27; Ezekiel 38:8,11; 1 Thessalonians 5:1–2; Revelation 6:1–2). The world will enter into a kind of new *Pax Romana* (Roman Peace).

5. In brokering the Middle East peace deal, the Antichrist will temporarily end the threat of terror and guarantee the uninterrupted flow of oil to the West. He will be hailed as a great peacemaker. At last, it will appear that the world has what it has waited for—peace and prosperity.

6. The world's utopia won't last long. Sometime during the first half of the tribulation, the coalition of nations in Ezekiel 38 will stage a surprise attack on Israel when she has let down her guard. Russia's expanding power and influence in the Middle East will be the hooks in the jaws that will drag her reluctantly into this course of action. The attack will be against both Israel and the West, since Israel will be joined to the Antichrist by her treaty. By this invasion of Israel, Iran and her allies will hope to draw the West into open confrontation— or a final great clash of civilizations.

7. God will supernaturally intervene, just like in Old Testament times, to miraculously rescue Israel from total annihilation and destroy the invaders.

8. The power vacuum created by the destruction of the armies of Russia, Iran, and most of the other Islamic nations will be quickly filled by the Antichrist. He will

seize this opportunity to launch his world empire at the midpoint of the seven-year tribulation. He will establish a headquarters in Babylon (modern Iraq) and seize control of the great oil supply in the Persian Gulf.

9. The Great Tribulation Jesus spoke of in Matthew 24:21 will break out, plunging the world into its final days of darkness and dismay.

10. The world will be saved from the brink of destruction by the Second Coming of Jesus Christ who will establish his 1,000-year kingdom of peace and righteousness on the earth.

You have to admit that it's quite a forecast. The earth appears to be on the verge of entering into its most dangerous and difficult days. This raises a very important, a very personal, question for every reader to face.

WHAT'S NEXT—FOR YOU?

In pondering the future of the world and our own future, the truth is that none of us knows how much time we have *personally* or *prophetically*.

Personally, we don't know if we will live to see tomorrow. God gives us no guarantee of another breath. Prophetically, the events of the end times may be much closer than many believe. Jesus could come today, and all who don't know Him will be left behind. The signs of the end are all around us, and while many people are searching for answers, most people are ignoring God's warnings.

On September 21, 1938, a hurricane of monstrous proportions struck the East Coast of the United States. William

Manchester, writing about it his book *The Glory and the Dream*, says that "the great wall of brine struck the beach between Babylon and Patchogue (Long Island, New York) at 2:30 p.m. So mighty was the power of that first storm wave that its impact registered on a seismograph in Sitka, Alaska, while the spray, carried northward at well over a hundred miles an hour, whitened windows in Montpelier, Vermont.

As the torrential 40-foot wave approached, some Long Islanders jumped into cars and raced inland. No one knows precisely how many lost that race for their lives, but the survivors later estimated that they had to keep the speedometer over 50 mph all the way. For some reason, the meteorologists—who should have known what was coming and should have warned the public—seemed strangely blind to the impending disaster. Either they ignored their instruments or simply couldn't believe them. And, of course, if the forecasters were blind, the public was too.

"Among the striking stories which later came to light," says Manchester, "was the experience of a Long Islander who had bought a barometer a few days earlier in a New York store. It arrived in the morning post September 21, and to his annoyance the needle pointed below 29, where the dial read, 'Hurricanes and Tornadoes.' He shook it and banged it against the wall; the needle wouldn't budge. Indignant, he repacked it, drove to the post office, and mailed it back. While he was gone, his house blew away."[108]

That's the way many people are today. If we can't cope with the forecast, we blame the barometer. Or ignore it. Or throw it away!

This may describe you right now. You see the signs all around you that a storm is coming, but you are trying to just ignore them. You are going on with your life. If so, then the most important thing for you to do is to hear God's Word and be saved from the wrath to come.

MAKE SURE YOU'RE READY

Are you ready to face the future? Are you prepared to meet the Lord when He comes? You can be. The Lord's plan for saving man from his sins is so easy that the Bible says we must become like a little child to enter God's kingdom. When you receive Christ personally as your Savior, you will immediately receive forgiveness for all your sins. For the very first time in your life, you will enter into a relationship with the living God.

Becoming a child of God involves three important steps.

STEP 1: Admit

You must realize that you need to be saved. You must admit your need. How many sins did it take for Adam and Eve to be excluded forever from the Garden of Eden? Just one. Likewise, it only takes one sin to keep us out of God's heaven. And if we are honest, we all know that we have committed many sins against the Lord. Romans 3:23 tells the truth about us. "For all have sinned and fall short of the glory of God."

STEP 2: Acknowledge

You must recognize and acknowledge that you need a Savior and that Jesus is the Savior you need. The Bible makes is clear that you cannot save yourself. No amount of good works, effort, church attendance, or ritual can take away your sin. "For by grace your have been saved through faith; and that not of yourselves, it is the gift of God; not as a result of works, so that no one may boast" (Ephesians 2:8–9). Jesus is the Son of God who died in your place on the cross and rose again on the third day. You can only be saved from your sins through Him. He is God's only way to heaven (John 14:6).

STEP 3: Accept

You must receive or accept Jesus Christ as your personal Savior from sin. It's not enough just to know that you are a sinner, that you need a Savior, and that Jesus is the Savior you need. You must personally receive Him by faith. You must accept Christ and what He has done for you. "But as many as received Him [Jesus], to them He gave the right to become children of God" (John 1:12).

NOW IS THE DAY OF SALVATION

Why not bow your head right now and call upon the Lord, accepting Christ as your personal Savior? Do it now. Don't put it off. When you receive Christ, God promises to give you the precious gift of eternal life. "He who believes in the Son has eternal life" (John 3:36).

There are no magic words that bring salvation. God knows your heart. But a simple prayer like this can be used to express your desire to accept Jesus Christ as your Savior who paid the price for your sins. If this prayer expresses the sincere desire of your heart to receive Christ as your personal Savior, God will save you right now. However and wherever you may be.

Lord, I admit that I'm a sinner,
and that I need a Savior. I know that I cannot save
myself. I believe that Jesus is the Son of God who
died on the cross for my sins and rose again from the dead.
I accept Him now to be my Savior and Lord. Thank you
for giving me the free gift of eternal life.

My sincerest prayer is that everyone who reads this book will be ready when Jesus comes to meet us in the air.

UNTIL HE COMES

If you have just received Christ, or if you have been a Christian for some time, you need to thank God again for His gracious gift of salvation and for calling you out of darkness into His marvelous light. In thankful response to God's grace, and as an obedient follower of Christ, you need to live in such a way that you are ready for the Lord to come at any moment.

Here are eight practical ways to stay alert, be ready, and grow and mature in your Christian life.

1. If you have never followed the Lord in believer's baptism, then you need to obey the Lord's command to be baptized in water (Matthew 28:19). Water baptism is to salvation what a wedding ring is to a marriage. It's not what makes you married, but rather it's the outward symbol that you are married.

2. Put away any known sin in your life. Turn from it today. Commit to being a pure vessel for the Lord to use (2 Timothy 2:20–22).

3. Confess any known sin in your life, so you can be restored in fellowship with the Lord (1 John 1:9). You can never lose your *relationship* with the Lord once you accept Christ, but you can fall out of *fellowship* with Him. Confession restores that interrupted fellowship.

4. Surrender your life each day to the control of the Holy Spirit. Now that you are a believer in Christ, the Holy Spirit has come to permanently indwell your life, but he will only fill you or control you as you yield to His will for your life (Ephesians 5:18).

5. Keep the lines of communication open between you and your heavenly Father in daily prayer (1 Thessalonians 5:17).

6. Find a good Bible-teaching, loving church to attend and support (Hebrews 10:25).

7. Use the gifts and abilities the Lord has given you to serve others (Matthew 25:14–30).

8. Look for, and live in light of, Christ's coming each day (Titus 2:13).

HOPE IN THE DARKNESS

There's no doubt that our world faces an unparalleled predicament. The storm clouds of the Iran crisis continue to gather around us. No human knows the details of how it will all play out or when the end will come. But I hope that you're convinced that God has revealed enough to help us see that what's happening right now is part of His master plan and that He's in control. There is no crisis with God. He knows all and controls all.

Never forget this great truth. Our God is the God of prophecy. He has revealed the future to give us confidence, peace, and hope in days of darkness.

My prayer for every reader is that you will be found in faith and faithful when the Savior comes.

A PROPOSED CHRONOLOGY OF THE END TIMES

n many of my books on end-times prophecy I like to include an outline at the end. I recognize that it's not easy trying to fit together all the pieces of the end times into a chronological sequence. I certainly wouldn't insist on the correctness of every detail in this outline, but my prayer is that it will help you get a better grasp of the overall flow of events in the end times.

I. EVENTS IN HEAVEN

    A. *The Rapture of the Church* (see 1 Corinthians 15:51–58; 1 Thessalonians 4:13–18; Revelation 3:10)

    B. *The Judgment Seat of Christ* (see Romans 14:10; 1 Corinthians 3:9–15; 4:1–5; 9:24–27; 2 Corinthians 5:10)

    C. *The Marriage of the Lamb* (see 2 Corinthians 11:2; Revelation 19:6–8)

    D. *The Singing of Two Special Songs* (see Revelation 4–5)

    E. *The Lamb Receiving the Seven-Sealed Scroll* (see Revelation 5)

II. EVENTS ON EARTH

    A. *Seven-Year Tribulation*

        1. Beginning of the Tribulation

    a. Seven-year Tribulation begins when the Antichrist signs a covenant with Israel, bringing peace to Israel and Jerusalem (see Daniel 9:27; Ezekiel 38:8, 11).

    b. The Jewish temple in Jerusalem is rebuilt (see Daniel 9:27; Revelation 11:1).

    c. The reunited Roman Empire emerges in a ten-leader configuration (see Daniel 2:40–44; 7:7; Revelation 17:12).

2. First Half (three and a half years) of the Tribulation

    a. The seven seal judgments are opened (see Revelation 6).

    b. The 144,000 Jewish believers begin their great evangelistic ministry (see Revelation 7).

    c. Gog and his allies invade Israel and are decimated by God (see Daniel 11:40–45; Ezekiel 38–39).

3. The Midpoint of the Tribulation

    a. Antichrist breaks his covenant with Israel and invades the Land (see Daniel 9:27; 11:40–41).

    b. Antichrist begins to consolidate his empire by plundering Egypt, Sudan, and Libya, whose armies have just been destroyed by God in Israel (see Daniel 11:42–43; Ezekiel 38–39).

    c. While in North Africa, Antichrist hears disturbing news of insurrection in Israel and immediately returns there to destroy and annihilate many (see Daniel 11:44).

    d. Antichrist sets up the abomination of desolation in the rebuilt temple in Jerusalem (see Daniel 9:27; 11:45a; Matthew 24:15; 2 Thessalonians 2:4; Revelation 13:5, 15–18).

    e. Sometime during these events, the Antichrist is violently killed, possibly as a result of a war or assassination (see Daniel 11:45; Revelation 13:3, 12, 14; 17:8).

f. Satan is cast down from heaven and begins to make war with Israel (see Revelation 12:7–13). The chief means he uses to persecute Israel is the two beasts in Revelation 13.

g. The faithful Jewish remnant flee to Petra in modern Jordan, where they are divinely protected for the remainder of the Tribulation (see Matthew 24:16–20; Revelation 12:15–17).

h. The Antichrist is miraculously raised from the dead to the awestruck amazement of the entire world (see Revelation 13:3).

i. After his resurrection from the dead, the Antichrist gains political control over the ten kings of the reunited Roman Empire. Three of these kings will be killed by the Antichrist, and the other seven will submit (see Daniel 7:24; Revelation 17:12–13).

j. The Two Witnesses begin their three-and-a-half-year ministry (see Revelation 11:3–6).

k. Antichrist and the ten kings destroy the religious system of Babylon and set up their religious capital in the city (see Revelation 17:16–17).

4. Last Half (three and a half years) of the Tribulation

a. Antichrist blasphemes God and the false prophet performs great signs and wonders and promotes false worship of the Antichrist (see Revelation 13:5, 11–15).

b. The mark of the beast (666) is introduced and enforced by the false prophet (see Revelation 13:16–18).

    c. Totally energized by Satan, the Antichrist dominates the world politically, religiously, and economically (see Revelation 13:4–5, 15–18).

    d. The trumpet judgments are unleashed throughout the final half of the Tribulation (see Revelation 8–9).

    e. Knowing he has only a short time left, Satan intensifies his relentless, merciless persecution of the Jewish people and Gentile believers on earth (see Daniel 7:25; Revelation 12:12; 13:15; 20:4).

5. The End of the Tribulation

    a. The bowl judgments are poured out in rapid succession (see Revelation 16).

    b. The Campaign of Armageddon begins (see Revelation 16:16).

    c. Commercial Babylon is destroyed (see Revelation 18).

    d. The two witnesses are killed by Antichrist and are resurrected by God three and a half days later (see Revelation 11:7–12).

    e. Christ returns to the Mount of Olives and slays the armies gathered against Him throughout the land, from Megiddo to Petra (see Revelation 19:11–16; Isaiah 34:1–6; 63:1–6).

    f. The birds gather to feed on the carnage (see Revelation 19:17–18).

B. *After the Tribulation*

1. Interval or Transition Period of Seventy-Five Days (see Daniel 12:12)

    a. The Antichrist and the false prophet are cast in the lake of fire (see Revelation 19:20–21).

b. The abomination of desolation is removed from the temple (see Daniel 12:11).

c. Israel is regathered (see Matthew 24:31).

d. Israel is judged (see Ezekiel 20:30–39; Matthew 25:1–30).

e. Gentiles are judged (see Matthew 25:31–46).

f. Satan is bound in the abyss (see Revelation 20:1–3).

g. Old Testament and Tribulation saints are resurrected (see Daniel 12:1–3; Isaiah 26:19; Revelation 20:4).

2. One-Thousand-Year Reign of Christ on Earth (see Revelation 20:4–6)

3. Satan's Final Revolt and Defeat (see Revelation 20:7–10)

4. The Great White Throne Judgment of the Lost (see Revelation 20:11–15)

5. The Destruction of the Present Heavens and Earth (see Matthew 24:35; 2 Peter 3:3–12; Revelation 21:1)

6. The Creation of the New Heavens and New Earth (see Isaiah 65:17; 66:22; 2 Peter 3:13; Revelation 21:1)

7. Eternity (see Revelation 21:9–22:5)

NOTES

1. William Kristol, "And Now Iran: We can't rule out the use of military force," *The Weekly Standard,* January 23, 2006, Vol. 011 Issue 18.
2. Nancy Gibbs, "Apocalypse Now," *Time,* July 1, 2002, p. 40.
3. Kenneth R. Timmerman, *Countdown to Crisis: The Coming Nuclear Showdown with Iran,* updated ed. (New York: Three Rivers Press, 2006), p. 331.
4. Louis Charbonneau, "Iran Said to Step Up Plans for Shahad Missiles," March 6, 2006, Reuters. See www.alertnet.org/thenews/newsdesk/L06200254.htm.
5. Ibid.
6. Christine Ollivier, "France Warns of Nuke Response to Terrorism," Associated Press, January 19, 2006. See news.yahoo.com/s/ap/2060119/ap_on_re_eu/france_nuclear, p. 1–2.
7. Graham Allison, *Nuclear Terrorism: The Ultimate Preventable Catastrophe* (New York: Owl Books, 2004), p. 161–62.
8. Barry R. Posner, "We Can Live With a Nuclear Iran," *The New York Times,* February 28, 2006.
9. CBS News, "Experts Warn of Future WMD Attack," June 22, 2005. See www.cbsnews.com/stories/2005/06/22/world/main/703465.shtml.
10. H. A. Ironside, *Lectures on Daniel the Prophet* (Neptune, NJ: Loizeaux Brothers, 1911), p. 117–18.
11. Mortimer B. Zuckerman, "Moscow's Mad Gamble," *U.S. News and World Report,* Internet Edition (January 30, 2006), p. 1.
12. Gary Sick, *All Fall Down: America's Fateful Encounter with Iran* (London: I. B. Tauris, 1985), p. 219.
13. Kenneth M. Pollack, *The Persian Puzzle: The Conflict Between Iran and America,* Trade Paperback Edition (New York: Random House Trade Paperbacks, 2005), p. 345.
14. Ibid. p. 282.
15. Ibid., p. 350–51.
16. Syed Saleem Shahzad, "Iran Takes Center Stage." *Asia Times Online,* January 22, 2002, 1–3. See www.atimes.com.
17. United States Department of State, *Patterns of Global Terrorism,* 2001.

18. Walid Phares, *Future Jihad* (New York: Palgrave Macmillan, 2005), p. 243.

19. Nicholas Kristof, *International Herald Tribune* (August 16, 2004).

20. Andrew C. McCarthy, "The War that Dare Not Speak Its Name: The battle is against militant Islam, not 'Terror,'" *National Review Online,* May 13, 2004.

21. Ibid.

22. Timmerman, *Countdown to Crisis,* p. 320.

23. "Iran urges worldwide Islamic revolt," *Iran News,* June 30, 2005. See www.irannewsdaily.com/v2/view_news.asp?id=119359.

24. *Daily News,* Vol XXVIII, No. 341, 24 February 2006. See www.gulf-daily-news.com/Story.asp?

25. Anton La Guardia, "Divine Mission Driving Iran's New Leader," January 14, 2006. See www.telegraph.co uk/news/main.jhtm

26. Timmerman, *Countdown to Crisis,* p. 325.

27. Arnaud de Borchgrave, "The Apocalyptic Vision of Iranian President Ahmadinejad," February 9, 2006. See www.newsmax.com/archives/articles/2006/2/8/154740.shtml.

28. Timmerman, *Countdown to Crisis,* p. 325.

29. Borchgrave, "The Apocalyptic Vision of Iranian President Ahmadinejad," p. 1.

30. Daniel Pipes, "The Mystical Menace of Mahmoud Ahmadinejad," *New York Sun,* January 10, 2006. See www.danielpipes.org/article/3258.

31. Zuckerman, "Moscow's Mad Gamble," p. 1.

32. Olasky, *World,* p. 21.

33. www.atomicarchive.com/.../iran_facilities.gif.

34. Louis Charbonneau, "Military Force Can't Destroy Our Atomic Program: Iran," Reuters, March 27, 2006. See http://today.reuters.com/news/newsArticle.aspx?type=topNews&storyI D=2006-03-27T145, p. 1.

35. *Associated Press,* April 23, 2006.

36. *The Daily Oklahoman,* April 25, 2005.

37. Thomas Ice, "Russia, Iran, and War Against Israel, *Pre-Trib Perspectives* (February 2006, vol 8, no. 31), p. 5.

38. Peter Tertzekian, *A Thousand Barrels a Second* (New York: McGraw-Hill, 2006), p. 125.

39. Ibid., p. 106.
40. Stephen Leeb, *The Coming Economic Collapse* (New York: Warner Business Books, 2006), p. 25.
41. Ibid., p. 27
42. Tertzekian, *A Thousand Barrels a Second*, p. 106.
43. Ibid., p. 90.
44. Richard J. Newman, "The Rise of a New Power," *U.S. News and World Report*, (6/20/05), p. 40.
45. "Reports: China, Iran Near Huge Oil Field Deal," Associated Press, February 17, 2006. See www.msnbc.msn.com/id/1140404589, p. 1.
46. Tertzakian, *One Thousand Barrels a Second*, p. 56.
47. George Gedda, "Poll: Americans See Iran as Enemy No. 1," Associated Press, February 24, 2006.
48. Philip Sherwell, "Pentagon Plan Strikes on Iran's Nuclear Plants," *The Sydney Morning Herald*, February 13, 2006. See www.smh.com.au/news/world/pentagon-plans-strikes-on-irans-nuclear-plants/2006/02/12/1139679479156.html.
49. William M. Arkin, "Early Warning." See blogs.washingtonpost.com/earlywarning/2006/03/attacking_iran_.html.
50. Allison, *Nuclear Terrorism*, p. 164.
51. Timmerman, *Countdown to Crisis*, p. 305.
52. Uzi Mahnaimi and Sarah Baxter, "Israel Readies Forces for Strike on Nuclear Iran," *Times Online*, December 11, 2005. See www.timesonline.co.uk/article/0,,2089-190074,00.html , p. 1.
53. Mahnaimi and Baxter, "Israel Readies Forces for Strike on Nuclear Iran," p. 2.
54. Pollack, *The Persian Puzzle*, p. 394.
55. Peggy Noonan, "What I Saw at the Devastation," *The Opinion Journal*, September 13, 2001. See www. Opinionjournal.com/columnists/pnoonan/?id=95001113, p. 1.
56. Allison, *Nuclear Terrorism*, p. 12.
57. Ibid., p. 15.
58. Olasky, "Nuke Nightmare," p. 20.
59. Ibid., p. 21.
60. "Two Years Later, the Fear Lingers," *Pew Research for the People and the Press*, September 4, 2003.
61. Allison, *Nuclear Terrorism*, p. 8, 228–29.

62. Ibid., p. 172.

63. Charles H. Dyer, *Rise of Babylon: Sign of the End Times* (Wheaton, IL: Tyndale House Publishers, 1991), p. 168.

64. Ibid., p. 214.

65. Rifkin, *The European Dream*, p. 200.

66. T. R. Reid, *The United States of Europe: The New Superpower and the End of American Supremacy* (New York: Penguin Books, 2004), p. 45–51.

67. Ibid., p. 51.

68. Ibid., p 1.

69. Ibid., p. 3. Rifkin, *The European Dream*, p. 61, 209–211.

70. Rifkin, *The European Dream*, p. 209.

71. Ibid., p. 385.

72. H. L. Willmington, *The King is Coming* (Wheaton, IL: Tyndale House Publishers, 1973), p. 95.

73. Samuel P. Huntington, *The Clash of Civilizations and the Remaking of the World Order* (New York: Simon and Schuster, 1996), p. 183.

74. John Piper, "Being Mocked," *World*, February 18, 2006, p. 43.

75. Ibid.

76. Clyde Billington notes the Akkadian tendency to drop or to change an initial "t" sound in a name especially if the initial "t" was followed by an "r" sound. If you drop the initial "T" from Tiras you are left with "ras." Clyde E. Billington Jr., "The Rosh People in History and Prophecy (Part Two)," *Michigan Theological Journal* 3 (1992): 66–67.

77. Arnold G. Fruchtenbaum, *The Footsteps of the Messiah*, rev. ed. (Tustin, CA: Ariel Press, 2003), p. 108.

78. Josephus *Antiquities* 1.6.1.

79. Concerning the possibility of a Russian/Islamic invasion of Israel in the end times, C. Marvin Pate and J. Daniel Hays say categorically, "The biblical term rosh has nothing to do with Russia." C. Marvin Pate and J. Daniel Hays, *Iraq–Babylon of the End Times?* (Grand Rapids: Baker Books, 2003), p. 69. And later they state dogmatically, "These positions are not biblical…. A world government is not coming to Babylon, and a Russian-led Muslim invasion of Israel is not about to take place" (ibid., p. 136).

80. Block, *Ezekiel 25–48*, p. 434.

81. The weight of evidence favors taking *Rosh* as a proper name in Ezekiel 38–39. There are four arguments that favor this view. First, the

eminent Hebrew scholars C. F. Keil and Wilhelm Gesenius both hold that the better translation of Rosh in Ezekiel 38:2-3 and 39:1 is as a proper noun referring to a specific geographical location C. F. Keil, *Ezekiel, Daniel, Commentary on the Old Testament*, trans. James Martin (Reprint; Grand Rapids: Eerdmans Publishing Company, 1982), p. 159. Wilhelm Gesenius, *Gesenius' Hebrew-Chaldee Lexicon to the Old Testament* (Reprint, Grand Rapids: Eerdmans Publishing Company, 1949), p. 752. Second, the *Septuagint*, which is the Greek translation of the Hebrew Old Testament, translates *Rosh* as the proper name *Ros* (*Rwj*). Third, many Bible dictionaries and encyclopedias, in their articles on Rosh, support taking it as a proper name in Ezekiel 38 such as New Bible Dictionary, Wycliffe Bible Dictionary, and International Standard Bible Encyclopedia. Fifth, the most impressive evidence in favor of taking Rosh as a proper name is simply that this translation is the most accurate. G. A. Cooke translates Ezekiel 38:2, "the chief of Rosh, Meshech and Tubal." He calls this "the most natural way of rendering the Hebrew." G. A. Cooke, *A Critical and Exegetical Commentary on the Book of Ezekiel*, International Critical Commentary, ed. S. R. Driver, A. Plummer, and C. A. Briggs (Edinburgh: T. & T. Clark, 1936), p. 408–9. For an extensive, thorough presentation of the grammatical and philological support for taking Rosh as a place name, see James D. Price "Rosh: An Ancient Land Known to Ezekiel," *Grace Theological Journal* 6 (1985): 67–89.

82. Gesenius, p. 752. In his original Latin version of the lexicon titled *Thesaurus Linguae Hebraeae et Chaldaeae Veteris Testamenti*, Gesenius has nearly one page of notes dealing with the word Rosh and the Rosh people mentioned in Ezekiel 38–39. This page of notes does not appear in any of the English translations of Gesenius' Lexicon. Those who disagree with Gesenius have failed to refute his sizable body of convincing evidence identifying Rosh with Russia.

83. Billington, "Rosh People (Part Two)," p. 145–46.

84. James D. Price, "Rosh: An Ancient Land Known to Ezekiel," *Grace Theological Journal* 6 (1985): 71–73.

85. Clyde E. Billington Jr., "The Rosh People in History and Prophecy (Part Three)," *Michigan Theological Journal* 4 (1993): 59, 61. Edwin Yamauchi is often quoted as the conclusive authority that Rosh cannot be Russia. He says that the name Rus, which the modern name Russia is based upon, "was brought into the region of Kiev, north of the Black

Sea, by the Vikings only in the Middle Ages." Edwin M. Yamauchi, *Foes from the Northern Frontier* (Grand Rapids: Baker Books, 1982), p. 20. However, while Yamauchi is a respected scholar, his conclusion stands in direct opposition to the substantial historical evidence presented by Wilhelm Gesenius, James Price, and Clyde Billington. For an excellent discussion of the relationship between Rosh and Russia, see Jon Mark Ruthven, *The Prophecy That is Shaping History: New Research on Ezekiel's Vision of the End* (Fairfax: VA: Xulon Press, 2003).

86. "The Kingdom of Kush," *National Geographic*, November 1990, p. 98–104.

87. Pollack, *The Persian Puzzle*, p. 256.

88. James B. Pritchard, ed., *Ancient Near Eastern Texts Relating to the Old Testament*, 3d ed. (Princeton: Princeton University Press, 1969), p. 308. Fruchtenbaum identifies Put as modern Somalia (*Footsteps of the Messiah*, p. 108).

89. *Brown-Driver-Briggs*, p. 806.

90. *The Cambridge Ancient History*, vol. 3, p. 510.

91. Yamauchi, *Foes from the Northern Frontier*, p. 49–52.

92. Josephus *Antiquities* 1.6.1.

93. In Ezekiel 39:2, the King James Version reads as if only five-sixths of the invading army will be destroyed. "And I will turn thee back, and leave but the sixth part of thee." However, most modern versions translate the Hebrew verb "lead thee on" (ASV), "drive you on" (NASB), "drag you along" (NIV), and "drive you" (NLT). These translations are preferred over the KJV. See Charles Lee Feinberg, *The Prophecy of Ezekiel* (Chicago: Moody Press, 1969), p. 228.

94. Clarence E. Mason Jr., "Gog and Magog, Who and When?" in *Prophecy in the Seventies*, ed. Charles Lee Feinberg (Chicago: Moody Press, 1971), p. 221.

95. Preterists, who believe that most or all of the prophecies in the Bible have already been fulfilled, contend that the events in Ezekiel 38–39 have already occurred. Gary DeMar argues strenuously for a "literal" interpretation of Ezekiel 38–39, and repeatedly criticizes Tim LaHaye and Jerry Jenkins for interpreting these chapters symbolically, thereby, spiritualizing the text. DeMar insists that Ezekiel 38–39 was "literally" fulfilled by the events described in Esther 9 occurring in about 473 BC in the days of Queen Esther of Persia. DeMar states that the parallels

between the battles in Ezekiel 38–39 and Esther are "unmistakable." Gary DeMar, *End Times Fiction: A Biblical Consideration of the Left Behind Theology* (Nashville, TN: Thomas Nelson Publishers, 2001), p. 12–15. DeMar, however, fails to account for several clear differences between Ezekiel 38–39 and Esther 9. A simple reading of the two passages reveals that they cannot possibly be describing the same event. Here are five of the more apparent and problematic inconsistencies.

Ezekiel 38–39	Esther 9
The land of Israel is invaded (38:16). The enemies fall on the mountains of Israel (39:4). Gog, the leader of the invasion, is buried in Israel (39:11)	Jews are attacked in cities throughout the Persian empire and defend themselves (9:2). The enemies die throughout the Persian empire.
The Jews bury the dead bodies over a period of seven months to cleanse the land of Israel (39:12)	No need to cleanse the land because the bodies are not in the land of Israel.
The invaders are destroyed by a massive earthquake in the land of Israel, infighting, plagues, and fire from heaven (38:19–22). God destroys the enemies supernaturally.	Attackers are killed by the Jewish people themselves assisted by local government leaders (9:3–5)
Invaders are from as far west as ancient Put (modern Libya) (Ezekiel 38:5) and as far north as Magog, the land of the Scythians.	The Persian empire never included these areas. It only extended as far west as Cush (modern Sudan) (Esther 8:9) and as far north as the southern part of the Black and Caspian Seas.
God sends fire upon Magog and those who inhabit the coastlands (39:6)	There is nothing even close to this in Esther 9.

One important question we might ask at this point is—if Ezekiel 38–39 was fulfilled in the events of Esther 9, why did this escape the notice of everyone in Esther's day? Why is there no mention in Esther of this great fulfillment of Ezekiel's prophecy? And why are there no Jewish scholars in that day or subsequently who recognized this fulfillment? The answer seems quite clear. Esther 9 did not fulfill Ezekiel 38–39. An important Jewish holiday known as Purim developed out of the Esther event (9:20–32). This is a joyous annual holiday to celebrate God's deliverance of Israel from the hand of her enemies. Purim's celebration includes the public reading of the book of Esther, but no tradition has developed or even been heard of in which the Jews read Ezekiel 38–39 in connection with this observance. If Ezekiel 38–39 had been fulfilled with Esther, then no doubt a tradition of reading that passage would have arisen in conjunction with the celebration.

96. The Hebrew word *'acharith* (end, last, or latter) when used in reference to time means "latter part" or "close." The standard Hebrew lexicon says, "in the end of the days, a prophetic phrase denoting the final period of the history so far as the speaker's perspective reaches… it often equals the ideal or Messianic future." *Brown-Driver-Briggs-Gesenius*, p. 31. Horst Seebass says that the Hebrew term "last days" or "end of the days" (*'acharith hayyamim*) is a technical term in Daniel 2:28; 10:14; Hosea 3:5, and Ezekiel 38:16 not just for the future in general but for the end of time. He says it refers to "how history will culminate, thus its outcome." Horst Seabass, *Theological Dictionary of the Old Testament*, ed. G. Johannes Botterweck and Helmer Ringgren, trans. John T. Willis (Grand Rapids: Eerdmans Publishing Company, 1974), p. 211–12.

97. John F. Walvoord, *The Nations in Prophecy* (Grand Rapids: Zondervan Publishing House, 1967), p. 105.

98. Tim LaHaye and Jerry B. Jenkins, *Left Behind* (Wheaton: Tyndale House Publishers, 1996), p. 9–10, 13–15.

99. *Brown-Driver-Briggs*, p. 1052-53.

100. Manfred Kober, "What is 'Gog and Magog' in Regard to Biblical Prophecy?" in *The Gathering Storm*, ed. Mal Couch (Springfield, MO: 21st Century Press, 2005), p. 174.

101. Walvoord, *Nations in Prophecy*, p. 113–15.

102. Ibid., p. 116.

103. Jon Mark Ruthven, *The Prophecy That is Shaping History: New Research on Ezekiel's Vision of the End* (Fairfax, VA: Xulon Press, 2003), p. 33.

104. W.A. Criswell, *Expository Sermons on the Book of Ezekiel* (Grand Rapids: Zondervan Publishing House, 1987), p. 212.

105. John F. Walvoord, *Israel in Prophecy*, rev. ed. (Grand Rapid, MI: Zondervan Publishing House, 1962), p. 129.
106. John F. Walvoord, *Armageddon, Oil and the Middle East Crisis*, rev. ed. (Grand Rapid, MI: Zondervan Publishing House, 1990), p. 227–28.
107. Ibid.
108. www.bible.org/illus.asp?topic_id=1666

ARE YOU CURIOUS WHETHER THE LEFT BEHIND SERIES IS TRUE TO THE BIBLE?

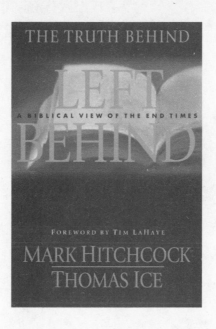

With the unparalleled worldwide success of the Left Behind series, both fans and critics are curious about the relationship between Bible prophecy and the events depicted in the novels. Responding to recent works that question Left Behind's biblical accuracy, two respected theologians set forth solid, biblical answers in this reader-friendly resource. Beginning with a clear presentation of prophecy interpretation and dispensationalism, the authors examine specific end times events represented in Left Behind and offer historical and biblical support for each event.

THE SUCCESSFUL END TIMES ANSWERS
SERIES PROVIDES READERS OF LEFT BEHIND
FICTION WITH A FACTUAL, BIBLICAL
UNDERSTANDING OF THE END TIMES
AND THE WORLD TODAY.

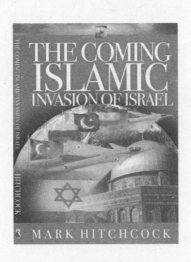

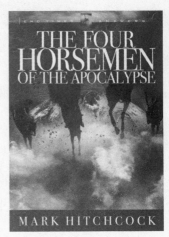

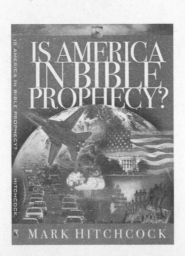

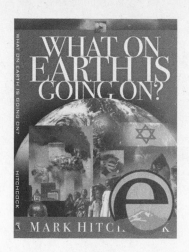

WHAT ON EARTH IS GOING ON?

MARK HITCHCOCK

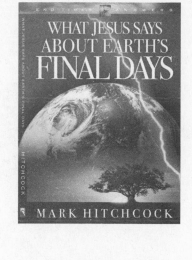

WHAT JESUS SAYS ABOUT EARTH'S FINAL DAYS

MARK HITCHCOCK

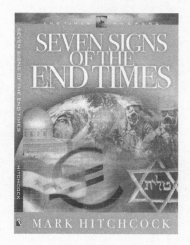

SEVEN SIGNS OF THE END TIMES

MARK HITCHCOCK

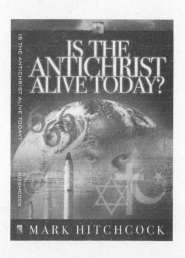

IS THE ANTICHRIST ALIVE TODAY?

MARK HITCHCOCK

THE END IS NEAR! OR IS IT?

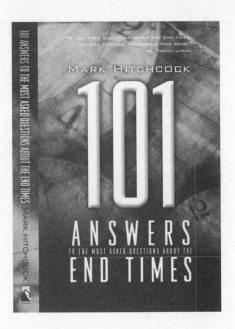

For many believers, the subject of the End Times stirs confusion, apprehension, and dread. No longer! This user-friendly manual answers 101 of the most frequently asked questions about everything from the Pre-Tribulation Rapture, the Antichrist, and Tribulation to the Second Coming and the Millennium. Prophecy expert Mark Hitchcock offers a biblically authoritative resource for understanding God's plan and a reason for peace instead of anxiety about each believer's role in it.

DEATH WILL NOT AVOID YOU!

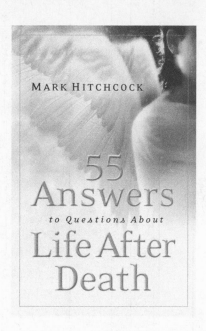

MARK HITCHCOCK

55
Answers
to Questions About
Life After
Death

Four thousand years ago, amid tragic suffering and death, Job asked the question of the ages: "If a man dies, will he live again?" Since the dawn of history, the subject of death and the afterlife has been the great question of human existence. It's a subject that everyone wonders about. What lies behind the veil of death? Is there really life after death? Is there a place called hell? This small yet power-packed book answers, in a very straightforward, reader-friendly format, all the most-asked questions ordinary people have about death, near-death experiences, cremation, purgatory, hell, heaven, and our future bodies. You'll be amazed at what awaits us beyond the grave.

GET CAUGHT UP IN THE RAPTURE!

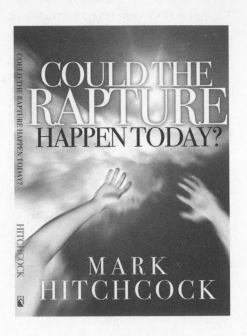

Religious jargon aside, just what is the rapture? Why is it such a big deal among Christians today? Here are the answers. *Could the Rapture Happen Today?* clearly defines this event and tackles the most commonly asked questions surrounding it. With solid evidence backing his responses, Mark Hitchcock also boldly explores the most controversial and pressing question, 'When will it happen?' With biblically sound, detailed arguments supporting the belief that the rapture will occur prior to the tribulation (pre-trib), Hitchcock tackles the question from every angle. Your nagging questions relieved, this fascinating page-turner will still leave you on the edge of your seat, anticipating Christ's return at any unexpected moment!

BABYLON IS A REAL PLACE.

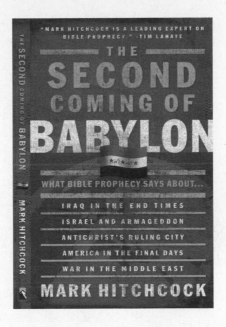

The Bible says that Babylon will be rebuilt and become the economic center of the world. Even now the ruins of the ancient city—just sixty miles south of Baghdad, Iraq—are quietly stirring. What does it mean for America? For Israel? For every person alive today? Are we living in the last days of earth as we know it? Find out, from Bible prophecy expert Mark Hitchcock... 1. How the focus of the world will shift back to Babylon 2. How Antichrist will make Babylon his capital 3. How the kingdoms of earth will fade as Babylon rises 4. How the false powers of Antichrist will grow 5. How prophecy will be fulfilled—and Babylon finally destroyed!